Tourism, Heritage Forests, and the Rights of Nature: Pathways to Sustainable Development in Iran

Atieh Mashayekhi

ISBN: 978-1-962443-17-3

DEDICATION

I dedicate this book to my beloved family, friends, and mentors, whose constant support, encouragement, and faith have been the foundation of my journey.

To the people of Iran, whose rich cultural heritage and natural beauty inspired the vision behind Tourism, Heritage Forests, and the Rights of Nature: Pathways to Sustainable Development in Iran.

Atieh Mashayekhi

CONTENTS

ACKNOWLEDGMENTS

The completion of this book, Tourism, Heritage Forests, and the Rights of Nature: Pathways to Sustainable Development in Iran, has been possible through the guidance, encouragement, and support of many individuals and institutions.

I extend my deepest gratitude to my mentors and colleagues whose insights and constructive feedback greatly enriched the quality of this work. I am thankful to the researchers, practitioners, and experts in tourism, sustainability, and environmental studies who generously shared their knowledge and experiences, which shaped the perspectives presented here.

Special thanks are due to my family and friends, whose patience, encouragement, and unwavering belief in me provided strength throughout this journey.

Finally, I express my respect and appreciation for the communities and custodians of Iran's heritage forests, whose voices and struggles inspired the central themes of this book. It is my hope that this work contributes in some measure to advancing the recognition of nature's rights and the pursuit of sustainable development.

Atieh Mashayekhi

CHAPTER 1

TOURISM, ENVIRONMENT, AND HERITAGE: CONCEPTUAL FOUNDATION

1.1 Tourism in the 21st Century
1.1.1 Global Importance of Tourism in the 21st Century

Tourism has emerged as one of the most dynamic sectors of the global economy, influencing not only economic growth but also cultural interaction and environmental policy. According to the United Nations World Tourism Organization (UNWTO), the number of international tourist arrivals surpassed 1.4 billion in recent years, and the sector contributes nearly 10% to global GDP. These figures underscore the magnitude of tourism as an economic driver, yet they only partially capture its societal and cultural significance. Tourism facilitates intercultural dialogue, enhances global awareness of heritage values, and promotes mutual understanding among nations, thereby playing a role in soft power and diplomacy (N. Khan et al., 2020).

At the same time, the expansion of tourism has intensified debates about its sustainability. The rapid growth of air travel, cruise tourism, and resort-based activities has amplified carbon emissions, resource consumption, and waste generation. This expansion often collides with the carrying capacity of destinations, overwhelming fragile ecosystems and cultural sites. For example, coastal tourism in Southeast Asia has generated significant revenue while simultaneously contributing to coral reef degradation and coastal erosion. The economic benefits of tourism, therefore, come with ecological and cultural trade-offs that require careful governance (Lachs & Oñate-Casado, 2020).

In this global context, heritage tourism occupies a central position. Tourists increasingly seek experiences connected to history, culture, and nature, leading to a rise in visits to World Heritage Sites, protected landscapes, and indigenous cultural areas. While this trend demonstrates a growing appreciation for heritage and environment, it also increases the risks of overuse and commercialization.

Thus, the global importance of tourism in the 21st century cannot be understood in isolation from environmental and heritage concerns. Instead, it must be seen as a complex system where economic, cultural, and ecological dimensions intersect (Bui et al., 2020).

1.1.2 Environment as the Foundation of Tourism

The environment constitutes the foundation upon which all tourism activities depend. Scenic landscapes, biodiversity, clean air, and healthy ecosystems form the "natural capital" that attracts visitors. Without the integrity of these resources, tourism loses its appeal and long-term viability. Forests, mountains, rivers, and wildlife are not simply passive settings for tourism; they are active elements that shape visitor experiences and national tourism identities. For instance, the tropical rainforests of Costa Rica, the savannas of Kenya, and the alpine landscapes of Switzerland serve as powerful images that define the tourism brand of these countries (Iskakova et al., 2021).

Yet, this foundation is highly vulnerable. Tourism development often requires infrastructure such as roads, hotels, and recreational facilities, which can disrupt ecosystems, fragment habitats, and introduce pollution. In fragile environments such as high-altitude forests or coastal wetlands, even modest tourism pressures can trigger irreversible ecological changes. The environmental footprint of tourism extends beyond the immediate destination, encompassing global challenges such as climate change. Aviation, a key enabler of international tourism, accounts for a significant share of carbon dioxide emissions, linking tourism growth to global warming (Leal Filho et al., 2023).

The interdependence between environment and tourism means that conservation is not merely an ethical choice but a practical necessity. Destinations that neglect environmental stewardship risk undermining the very resources that sustain their tourism industries. Conversely, destinations that integrate conservation into tourism planning can achieve a form of synergy where economic benefits support ecological protection. Examples include eco-lodges in the Amazon that fund biodiversity research, or community-based tourism projects in Nepal that link forest protection with income generation. These models demonstrate that safeguarding the environment is essential to securing the future of tourism (Nepal et al., 2022).

1.1.3 Heritage as a Bridge Between Past and Future

Heritage is not a static collection of monuments or artifacts; it is a living bridge that connects societies to their past while shaping their vision for the future. The concept of heritage has expanded significantly over recent decades, moving beyond tangible assets such as historic buildings and archaeological sites to include natural landscapes, forests, rivers, and intangible cultural practices. This broader understanding, codified in UNESCO's definitions of cultural and natural heritage, reflects the recognition that identity and memory are embedded not only in material structures but also in ecosystems and traditions. Forests, for example, are often intertwined with indigenous narratives, rituals, and livelihoods, making them cultural as well as ecological treasures (Akalibey et al., 2024).

Natural heritage in the form of forests exemplifies this dual role. Forest ecosystems are vital for biodiversity, carbon storage, and climate regulation, but they are also deeply symbolic spaces where human communities have developed myths, religions, and practices over centuries. The Hyrcanian Forests of Iran illustrate this duality vividly. These ancient forests, dating back 25–50 million years, are not only ecological relics of the Tertiary period but also cultural landscapes that have shaped the lives and imaginations of local communities. As UNESCO notes, they represent an irreplaceable record of ecological and evolutionary history, while for Iranians they embody a living connection to ancestral traditions and regional identity (Trajkovska Petkoska et al., 2025).

This dual significance, however, renders heritage especially vulnerable in the context of tourism. While recognition as a World Heritage Site or protected forest can enhance conservation efforts, it also increases exposure to mass visitation, commercialization, and political instrumentalization. Heritage thus faces the paradox of needing to be both preserved and made accessible. The task for policymakers and scholars is to develop frameworks that allow heritage to function as a bridge between past and future maintaining its integrity while enabling sustainable use. In this sense, heritage forests are not simply natural assets but also cultural legacies that demand careful stewardship for the benefit of present and future generations (Rollo, 2025).

1.1.4 The Paradox of Tourism and Sustainability

Tourism has long been celebrated as a tool for economic development, cultural exchange, and environmental awareness. By generating revenue and employment, it provides governments and local communities with the financial resources needed for conservation initiatives. Entrance fees to national parks, community-based ecotourism programs, and heritage site preservation funds are examples of how tourism can directly contribute to environmental protection. Moreover, exposure to natural and cultural heritage can foster greater appreciation among visitors, reinforcing public support for conservation policies. In theory, tourism thus represents a pathway toward sustainability,

where economic activity and environmental protection reinforce one another
(A. Khan et al., 2020).

In practice, however, the expansion of tourism often undermines the very
resources it depends upon. Mass tourism brings with it a range of
environmental pressures, from deforestation and soil erosion to water pollution
and waste accumulation. The phenomenon of overtourism where visitor
numbers exceed the carrying capacity of destinations has become a critical issue
in globally renowned sites. Cities such as Venice and Barcelona struggle with
infrastructure strain and loss of local identity, while natural sites like Machu
Picchu face physical erosion from excessive foot traffic. Iran is not immune to
this paradox: in the Hyrcanian Forests, tourism has introduced solid waste
pollution, habitat disturbance, and pressures on fragile ecosystems, despite the
forest's designation as a UNESCO World Heritage Site (Ghorbani et al., 2023).

This paradox lies at the heart of sustainability debates in tourism. While
tourism is promoted as a solution to conservation financing and rural
development, its unchecked growth often exacerbates ecological vulnerability
and cultural commodification. The challenge is to navigate between these
contradictory outcomes by designing governance systems that balance access
with protection. Concepts such as carrying capacity, limits of acceptable change,
and sustainable tourism indicators are attempts to resolve this paradox in
practice. Yet, the persistence of degradation at many heritage sites reveals that
theoretical frameworks are often insufficient without strong political will,
community involvement, and long-term planning. The paradox of tourism and
sustainability, therefore, is not merely a technical issue but a deeply political and
ethical one, requiring a rethinking of how societies value and manage their
natural and cultural heritage (Bridgewater & Rotherham, 2019).

1.1.5 The Emergence of Rights of Nature

The Rights of Nature (RoN) is one of the most innovative and radical
frameworks to emerge in contemporary environmental thought. Traditionally,
environmental governance has been dominated by anthropocentric
perspectives, treating nature primarily as a resource for human use and
economic growth. In contrast, the RoN framework argues that ecosystems,
species, and landscapes have intrinsic rights to exist, thrive, and regenerate,
regardless of their utility to human societies. This perspective is deeply
influenced by indigenous worldviews, where rivers, forests, and mountains are
often regarded as living entities with spiritual and moral significance. By
challenging the dominant paradigm, RoN provides a profound shift in how
societies conceptualize their relationship with the environment (Upreti, 2023).

This approach has moved beyond theory and entered the realm of law and policy. Ecuador's 2008 Constitution was the first in the world to explicitly recognize the rights of nature, granting ecosystems the legal right to exist and be restored. Bolivia followed with the "Law of the Rights of Mother Earth" in 2010, and New Zealand granted legal personhood to the Whanganui River and Te Urewera Forest, enabling indigenous communities to act as guardians of these natural entities. These legal innovations have attracted global attention, sparking debates about whether RoN can offer more effective protections for ecosystems than conventional conservation models. Proponents argue that granting nature legal rights can help counterbalance extractive industries and short-term development pressures, while critics caution about implementation challenges and conflicts with existing property regimes (Collins et al., 2019).

Although Iran has not formally adopted the Rights of Nature in its legal or policy frameworks, the concept holds significant relevance for the country's heritage forests and tourism sector. Iran's Hyrcanian and Zagros forests face pressures from deforestation, urban expansion, and poorly managed tourism. Introducing RoN as a normative if not yet legal framework could help reframe debates about their protection. By recognizing forests as entities with intrinsic rights, Iranian policymakers, conservationists, and tourism planners could move beyond utilitarian arguments and embrace a more Eco-friendly approach. Such a perspective would not only align Iran with global sustainability discourses but also resonate with cultural and religious traditions that emphasize stewardship of the natural world. In this way, the Rights of Nature provides both a philosophical lens and a practical tool for rethinking tourism and environmental governance in the Iranian context (Ghaderi et al., 2025).

1.1.6 Scope and Structure of the Chapter

This chapter provides the conceptual foundation for examining the interconnected themes of tourism, environment, heritage, and the emerging discourse on the Rights of Nature. Its scope is deliberately broad, reflecting the global significance of these issues and their particular resonance for Iran. By beginning with the global importance of tourism in the twenty-first century, the chapter situates Iran's challenges within wider international debates, demonstrating that concerns about environmental sustainability, heritage preservation, and ethical governance are not unique to one country but part of a shared global agenda. This broad lens helps highlight both the opportunities and risks that tourism brings to environments and heritage landscapes.

The chapter is organized around key thematic areas that together form an integrated framework. It begins with a discussion of the interdependent realities of tourism and the environment, emphasizing the central role of ecosystems in sustaining tourism activities. It then examines the notion of heritage as a bridge between past and future, expanding the concept beyond monuments to include forests and cultural landscapes. The paradox of tourism and sustainability is explored next, highlighting the contradictions between economic benefits and ecological costs. Finally, the Rights of Nature is introduced as a normative framework that challenges anthropocentric governance models and offers fresh perspectives for rethinking tourism's relationship with the environment. This progression ensures that readers move from general considerations to more innovative and transformative concepts.

In setting this conceptual foundation, the chapter also establishes a roadmap for the rest of the book. The following chapters will build on these themes by applying them directly to the Iranian context. Chapter 2 will analyze Iran's heritage forests, exploring their ecological and cultural values. Chapter 3 will examine the environmental challenges of tourism in these forests, while Chapter 4 will consider the potential of Rights of Nature as a guiding framework for sustainable tourism governance. Chapter 5 will then bring together policy recommendations, practical strategies, and future perspectives. By linking global debates with Iranian realities, this structure allows the book to move from theory to application, providing insights that are academically rigorous and practically relevant.

1.2 Tourism and the Environment: Interdependent Realities

1.2.1 Tourism as a Driver of Environmental Change

Tourism is often described as a double-edged sword in environmental discourse. On one side, it functions as a powerful driver of economic growth, local development, and cultural exchange. On the other, it exerts significant pressure on natural systems through land use, resource consumption, and waste generation. The environmental changes triggered by tourism are not uniform; they vary depending on the type of tourism, the fragility of ecosystems, and the governance structures in place. Mass tourism, characterized by large numbers of visitors and infrastructure-intensive development, typically exerts greater environmental stress compared to small-scale, community-based, or eco-oriented tourism (Koot, 2019).

The expansion of tourism infrastructure such as hotels, resorts, airports, and roads frequently involves the conversion of forests, wetlands, and coastal zones into built environments. This process results in habitat fragmentation, biodiversity loss, and soil degradation. Tourism-driven urbanization also accelerates water and energy consumption, often exceeding the carrying capacity of destinations. For instance, popular Mediterranean resorts face

chronic water shortages in the summer months, when tourist demand peaks
and local resources are already under stress (Skrimizea & Parra, 2019).

Equally important is the global dimension of tourism as a driver of
environmental change. International air travel, cruise tourism, and road
transportation collectively contribute a significant share of global carbon
emissions. According to the International Air Transport Association (IATA),
aviation alone accounts for around 2–3% of global CO_2 emissions, and
tourism-related mobility continues to grow. Thus, while tourism is celebrated
as a "smokeless industry," its carbon footprint reveals a less benign reality. In
this sense, tourism cannot be separated from broader debates about climate
change, energy transitions, and environmental justice (Tehseen et al., 2024).

1.2.2 Positive and Negative Environmental Impacts of Tourism

The impacts of tourism on the environment are complex and ambivalent.
On the positive side, tourism has the potential to generate significant resources
for conservation. Entrance fees, eco-taxes, and community-based tourism
projects can provide steady income streams for protected areas and local
populations. In some cases, tourism incentivizes governments to preserve
forests, wetlands, and wildlife habitats that might otherwise be converted to
agricultural or industrial uses. Ecotourism initiatives in Costa Rica, for example,
have helped finance national parks and create employment opportunities while
raising international awareness about biodiversity protection (Janzen &
Hallwachs, 2020).

Tourism can also contribute to environmental education. When visitors
engage in guided tours, interpretation programs, or community-based
experiences, they often leave with a greater appreciation of ecological and
cultural heritage. This awareness can translate into broader support for
conservation efforts, both locally and globally. Moreover, tourism can empower
indigenous and rural communities by creating alternative livelihoods that align
with environmental stewardship, reducing reliance on extractive practices such
as logging or poaching (Gaodirelwe et al., 2020).

Yet, the negative impacts of tourism are often more immediate and visible.
Overcrowding at popular sites leads to soil compaction, vegetation loss, and
wildlife disturbance. In forest ecosystems, poorly managed trails and camping
sites result in erosion, pollution, and habitat degradation. The proliferation of
plastic waste water bottles, food packaging, and single-use items—is a persistent
problem in both developed and developing contexts. Furthermore, cultural
landscapes are vulnerable to commodification, where traditions are simplified
or staged for tourist consumption, eroding their authenticity. In Iran's heritage

forests, for instance, unregulated picnicking and littering have created serious challenges, despite widespread public concern for environmental sustainability (Madani et al., 2024).

The duality of tourism's impacts highlights the need for governance frameworks that maximize benefits while minimizing harm. Tools such as carrying capacity assessments, environmental impact studies, and sustainability indicators can guide decision-making. However, these tools are effective only when combined with community participation, political will, and long-term vision. Without these, tourism risks tipping the balance toward degradation rather than protection (Cheer et al., 2019).

1.2.3 Global Case Studies on Tourism–Environment Interactions

Case studies from around the world demonstrate the diversity of tourism's environmental impacts and the importance of context in shaping outcomes. In Bhutan, a "high-value, low-impact" tourism policy restricts visitor numbers and charges a daily sustainability fee, ensuring that tourism revenues are reinvested into conservation and social development. This model has helped protect fragile mountain ecosystems while maintaining cultural integrity. By contrast, destinations like Bali have experienced uncontrolled tourism growth, leading to water scarcity, waste crises, and the loss of traditional agricultural landscapes. These contrasting examples illustrate that policy design is as crucial as natural endowment in determining environmental outcomes (Massenberg et al., 2023).

In Latin America, Costa Rica provides a well-documented case of how ecotourism can contribute to conservation. By positioning itself as a biodiversity hotspot and marketing its national parks, Costa Rica has generated significant revenue for conservation and rural development. However, even here, challenges remain: infrastructure expansion and rising tourist numbers pose risks of overuse, showing that ecotourism is not immune to sustainability dilemmas. Similarly, in Africa, wildlife tourism in Kenya and Tanzania has created economic incentives for preserving savannas and wildlife populations. Yet, these initiatives sometimes conflict with local land rights and fuel debates over equity and access (Croker et al., 2023).

Iran offers its own instructive cases. The Hyrcanian Forests, now inscribed as a UNESCO World Heritage Site, have seen a rise in domestic tourism, particularly during holidays. While this has increased public appreciation for the forests, it has also resulted in uncontrolled waste disposal, habitat disturbance, and pressure on local infrastructure. The Zagros Forests face similar tensions, where traditional pastoralist practices intersect with new tourism activities, raising questions about resource management and community participation.

These Iranian examples reflect the global paradox: tourism can both elevate the value of heritage environments and accelerate their degradation when not properly managed (Abouei & Tavasoli, 2024).

1.3 Understanding Heritage in the Context of Tourism

1.3.1 Defining Heritage: Cultural, Natural, and Mixed Dimensions

Heritage is a multi-dimensional concept that encompasses the tangible and intangible legacies of human societies and the natural environment. Traditionally, heritage was associated primarily with monumental architecture, archaeological sites, and works of art that symbolized cultural achievement. However, the twentieth century witnessed a broadening of this definition to include natural landscapes, biodiversity, and cultural practices. The UNESCO World Heritage Convention (1972) crystallized this expanded view by recognizing both "cultural heritage" and "natural heritage," while also allowing for "mixed sites" that embody both ecological and cultural values. This holistic understanding underscores the interdependence of human societies and their environments (Cárcamo Macoto et al., 2024).

Cultural heritage includes monuments, historic towns, traditional practices, and intangible elements such as music, rituals, and oral traditions. Natural heritage encompasses forests, rivers, mountains, and other ecosystems that possess outstanding universal value. Mixed heritage sites, such as sacred forests or cultural landscapes, embody both dimensions, reflecting centuries of interaction between humans and nature. For example, the rice terraces of the Philippine Cordilleras illustrate how human ingenuity can work with ecological conditions to create sustainable landscapes that are both functional and culturally significant (Paing et al., 2022).

This expanded definition of heritage has profound implications for tourism. By recognizing natural landscapes and living traditions as heritage, tourism becomes a vehicle not only for cultural exchange but also for environmental appreciation and protection. At the same time, it complicates the management of heritage, since safeguarding a living forest or a cultural practice involves different strategies than maintaining a static monument. Heritage in tourism, therefore, requires flexible and context-sensitive approaches that acknowledge both ecological processes and cultural dynamics (Wang & Fouseki, 2025).

1.3.2 Forests as Living Heritage Landscapes

Forests are increasingly recognized as more than reservoirs of biodiversity they are also cultural and spiritual landscapes that embody collective memory and identity. For many indigenous and rural communities, forests are sacred spaces where rituals are performed, myths are told, and livelihoods are sustained. These cultural associations transform forests into "living heritage," where ecological and cultural values are inseparable. The concept of cultural landscapes, endorsed by UNESCO, captures this dual role by highlighting places where human activity and natural processes have co-evolved over centuries (Løland & Akman, 2025).

The Hyrcanian Forests of Iran are a prime example of this phenomenon. Stretching along the Caspian Sea, these forests are ecological relics that date back millions of years, sheltering unique plant and animal species. But they are also interwoven with human history: local communities have long relied on them for medicinal plants, timber, and cultural practices such as Nowruz rituals. The forests thus embody both natural and cultural heritage, making them invaluable not only for biodiversity conservation but also for sustaining cultural traditions (Rollo, 2025).

Tourism adds another layer to this dynamic. Visitors are drawn to forests for their aesthetic beauty, recreational opportunities, and cultural symbolism. However, this very attraction creates pressures waste accumulation, trail erosion, and disturbance of wildlife that threaten the integrity of forests as heritage landscapes. The challenge lies in developing tourism strategies that allow visitors to experience the cultural and ecological richness of forests without compromising their long-term viability. This requires careful planning, local participation, and frameworks that treat forests as living entities rather than static resources (Tampekis et al., 2024).

1.3.3 Heritage, Identity, and Collective Memory

Heritage functions as a repository of identity, shaping how communities understand themselves and their place in the world. Cultural practices, historic sites, and natural landscapes often serve as symbols of continuity, linking generations through shared memory. Forests, in particular, are imbued with stories, myths, and rituals that reinforce social cohesion. In many societies, sacred groves or holy trees embody spiritual beliefs, acting as physical manifestations of cultural memory. The loss of such landscapes can therefore represent not only ecological degradation but also cultural erosion (Fairclough, 2019).

In Iran, forests play a significant role in national and regional identity. The Hyrcanian Forests are celebrated as "green jewels" of the Caspian region, while the Zagros Forests are associated with nomadic pastoralism and traditional knowledge systems. These forests are more than ecological spaces they are symbolic anchors of cultural heritage that contribute to a sense of belonging.

Tourism amplifies this symbolic role by showcasing forests to domestic and international visitors, reinforcing their value as national treasures (Melaku & Pastor Ivars, 2024).

Yet, the relationship between heritage and identity is not without tensions. Tourism can commodify cultural practices, reducing rituals or traditions to staged performances for visitors. Similarly, forests may be marketed primarily as tourist attractions, neglecting their deeper cultural meanings. This tension raises important ethical questions: how can heritage be presented to tourists without eroding its authenticity? Addressing this requires participatory tourism models that empower local communities to control how their heritage is interpreted and shared, ensuring that tourism strengthens rather than undermines cultural identity (Scheyvens & van der Watt, 2021).

1.3.4 The Challenges of Heritage Tourism Management

Managing heritage in the context of tourism is a complex endeavor that requires balancing accessibility with preservation. Unlike monuments, which can be fenced off or restricted, forests and cultural landscapes are living systems that evolve over time. Tourism planning must therefore account for ecological dynamics, cultural practices, and community needs. Tools such as carrying capacity assessments, heritage impact assessments, and community-based management models have been developed to address these challenges. However, their implementation varies widely across contexts, often depending on political will and institutional capacity (Siegel & Lima, 2020).

One of the most pressing challenges is overtourism, where visitor numbers exceed the ability of heritage sites to absorb them without damage. In natural heritage areas, this leads to soil compaction, vegetation loss, and wildlife disturbance. In cultural contexts, overtourism disrupts local communities and erodes traditional practices. The global COVID-19 pandemic highlighted the vulnerability of heritage tourism to external shocks, with closures of sites revealing both the dependence of communities on tourism income and the temporary ecological relief that reduced visitation provided (Bhammar et al., 2021).

For Iran, these challenges are particularly acute. The Hyrcanian Forests, despite their World Heritage status, face limited infrastructure for waste management, visitor education, and community engagement. Similarly, the Zagros Forests suffer from deforestation, overgrazing, and climate stress, compounded by rising tourism. Addressing these challenges requires integrating international best practices with local knowledge, ensuring that heritage tourism becomes a tool for resilience rather than degradation (Bui et al., 2020).

1.4 Global Frameworks for Heritage Protection

1.4.1 The UNESCO World Heritage Convention (1972)

The UNESCO World Heritage Convention, adopted in 1972, represents the most influential global framework for the protection of heritage. It established the principle of "outstanding universal value" as the benchmark for designating cultural and natural sites of global significance. By creating the World Heritage List, the convention sought not only to preserve sites of exceptional importance but also to raise awareness about the interconnectedness of heritage across national boundaries. Today, over 1,100 sites have been inscribed, spanning cultural monuments, historic cities, natural ecosystems, and mixed cultural–natural landscapes (O'Reilly, 2020).

The convention's significance lies not only in the symbolic recognition of heritage but also in its ability to mobilize international support. Inscription on the World Heritage List brings global visibility, technical expertise, and access to conservation funding through mechanisms such as the World Heritage Fund. However, it also imposes responsibilities on states to safeguard their sites, requiring the preparation of management plans and periodic reporting. In this sense, UNESCO functions both as a promoter and as a guardian, holding states accountable for the long-term sustainability of their heritage (Rosetti et al., 2022).

Iran has actively engaged with the World Heritage framework, securing the inscription of several cultural and natural sites, including the Hyrcanian Forests in 2019. This recognition has elevated the profile of Iran's forests, positioning them within a global conservation discourse. Yet, inscription is only the beginning: without effective domestic management, World Heritage status may attract mass tourism that overwhelms fragile ecosystems. Thus, while UNESCO provides a powerful framework for heritage protection, its effectiveness depends on how states integrate its principles into national policies and practices (Jagielska-Burduk et al., 2021).

1.4.2 The International Union for Conservation of Nature (IUCN) and World Heritage Forests

The International Union for Conservation of Nature (IUCN) plays a central role in global conservation by bridging science, policy, and practice. As an advisory body to UNESCO on natural heritage, the IUCN evaluates nominations of natural sites for World Heritage status and monitors their condition. Its assessments are grounded in scientific expertise and reflect a commitment to biodiversity conservation, ecosystem services, and climate resilience. Beyond its work with UNESCO, the IUCN also develops the Red

List of Threatened Species, protected area categories, and global standards for conservation planning (Betts et al., 2020).

Forests occupy a prominent place in IUCN's agenda. The organization has repeatedly emphasized that World Heritage forests—covering over 69 million hectares across the globe—are critical for biodiversity, carbon sequestration, and cultural identity. Reports by the IUCN have documented how these forests mitigate climate change, support millions of people's livelihoods, and safeguard species found nowhere else. However, they also face threats from illegal logging, agricultural expansion, mining, and poorly managed tourism. These pressures highlight the gap between legal protection and practical enforcement (Sharma, 2025).

For Iran, IUCN's role is highly relevant in guiding conservation strategies for the Hyrcanian and Zagros forests. By aligning national forest management with IUCN's scientific frameworks, Iran can strengthen both ecological and cultural resilience. Moreover, IUCN's emphasis on integrating local communities into conservation resonates with Iran's rural and indigenous practices, where forest stewardship has historically been embedded in social and cultural systems. Thus, the IUCN framework not only complements UNESCO's recognition but also provides the scientific and practical tools necessary for effective heritage forest management (Liburd & Becken, 2020).

1.4.3 The Global Sustainable Tourism Council (GSTC) Criteria

While UNESCO and IUCN focus primarily on heritage conservation, the Global Sustainable Tourism Council (GSTC) addresses the tourism dimension of sustainability. Established in 2007, GSTC has developed a set of global standards for sustainable tourism, known as the GSTC Criteria. These criteria serve as a framework for destinations, tour operators, and accommodations to assess and improve their sustainability practices. They cover four main pillars: sustainable management, socio-economic benefits for local communities, cultural heritage preservation, and environmental stewardship (Hariram et al., 2023).

The GSTC framework is particularly valuable because it translates abstract principles of sustainability into practical indicators. For instance, it emphasizes minimizing negative environmental impacts, reducing waste and water consumption, conserving biodiversity, and respecting local traditions. Certification programs based on the GSTC Criteria provide destinations with international recognition, helping them attract environmentally conscious tourists. At the same time, the criteria encourage governments and businesses to adopt long-term strategies rather than focusing solely on short-term gains (Orîndaru et al., 2021).

In the Iranian context, the GSTC Criteria could play an important role in shaping tourism policies for heritage forests. At present, many forest tourism activities in Iran are informal and lack systematic regulation, leading to problems such as waste accumulation and habitat disturbance. By adopting GSTC-aligned practices, Iran could establish clearer standards for sustainable forest tourism, enhance visitor education, and involve local communities in decision-making. Integrating the GSTC framework with UNESCO and IUCN principles would create a comprehensive approach where conservation and tourism development reinforce one another.

1.5 Sustainable Tourism: Principles and Practices

1.5.1 Evolution of the Sustainable Tourism Concept

The concept of sustainable tourism emerged in response to growing concerns about the environmental and cultural impacts of mass tourism. Initially, tourism development in the mid-twentieth century was driven by economic priorities, with little regard for ecological limits or cultural integrity. The rise of mass tourism in Europe, North America, and parts of Asia in the 1960s and 1970s exemplified this trend, leading to rapid coastal urbanization, the decline of traditional livelihoods, and ecological degradation. By the 1980s, however, scholars and policymakers began to recognize that unchecked tourism growth was unsustainable, prompting calls for new frameworks that could balance development with preservation (Khater et al., 2024).

The publication of the Brundtland Report in 1987, which popularized the concept of "sustainable development," provided a foundation for sustainable tourism. It emphasized intergenerational equity and the need to integrate environmental and social considerations into development planning. Tourism researchers quickly adapted this framework, arguing that tourism should not only generate short-term economic benefits but also safeguard ecosystems and cultural heritage for future generations. The 1992 Rio Earth Summit further reinforced these ideas by calling for global action on biodiversity, climate change, and sustainable resource use, with tourism identified as both a problem and a potential solution (Hariram et al., 2023).

Since then, sustainable tourism has evolved from a theoretical concept into a practical agenda adopted by governments, NGOs, and private businesses. International organizations such as the UNWTO, UNEP, and UNESCO have promoted sustainable tourism guidelines, while certification schemes and voluntary codes of conduct have proliferated. Despite these advances, debates persist over whether sustainable tourism is genuinely transformative or merely a rhetorical tool. Critics argue that the term is often used to legitimize tourism growth without addressing fundamental contradictions, while advocates insist that it remains the best framework for reconciling tourism with environmental and cultural stewardship (Liburd & Becken, 2020).

1.5.2 Ecotourism and Nature-Based Tourism

Among the various forms of sustainable tourism, ecotourism has gained particular prominence. Defined as responsible travel to natural areas that conserves the environment and improves the well-being of local people, ecotourism emerged in the late twentieth century as both a niche market and a philosophy of tourism. Unlike mass tourism, which prioritizes convenience and entertainment, ecotourism emphasizes small-scale, low-impact activities such as wildlife observation, trekking, and community engagement. Advocates argue that ecotourism generates financial incentives for conservation while promoting environmental education among visitors (Wani et al., 2025).

Nature-based tourism extends these principles to a broader set of activities, including adventure tourism, birdwatching, and forest recreation. It is one of the fastest-growing segments of the global tourism industry, reflecting a rising demand for authentic experiences in natural environments. Countries like Costa Rica, Kenya, and Nepal have successfully marketed themselves as destinations for nature-based tourism, integrating conservation goals with national branding strategies. However, even ecotourism and nature-based tourism are not without risks. Poorly managed ecotourism can lead to habitat disturbance, cultural exploitation, and inequitable distribution of benefits, undermining its sustainability objectives (Baloch et al., 2023).

In the Iranian context, ecotourism has significant potential, particularly in heritage forests such as the Hyrcanian and Zagros ecosystems. These areas offer unique opportunities for trekking, birdwatching, and cultural immersion. Yet, most tourism in these forests remains informal, with limited regulation and infrastructure. Ecotourism could provide an alternative to mass visitation if developed with strong community participation and adherence to international best practices. By positioning heritage forests as ecotourism destinations, Iran could simultaneously strengthen conservation, diversify its tourism industry, and align itself with global sustainability discourses (Ghorbani et al., 2023).

1.5.3 Carrying Capacity and Limits of Acceptable Change

One of the central principles of sustainable tourism is the recognition of ecological and social limits. The concept of carrying capacity refers to the maximum number of visitors that a site can accommodate without causing unacceptable levels of environmental degradation or social disruption. Originally developed in ecology to describe population limits in ecosystems, the concept was adapted to tourism in the 1970s and 1980s. It provided managers with a framework for regulating visitation, infrastructure development, and resource use (Page & Connell, 2020).

However, carrying capacity has been criticized for being overly rigid and difficult to measure. Determining a precise number of "acceptable" visitors often overlooks the complexity of ecosystems and the variability of human behavior. In response, scholars and practitioners developed the concept of Limits of Acceptable Change (LAC), which emphasizes qualitative thresholds rather than fixed numbers. LAC shifts the focus from how many tourists can be accommodated to what kinds of changes are acceptable, based on stakeholder input, monitoring, and adaptive management. This approach allows for more flexible and participatory decision-making (Zuniga-Teran et al., 2022).

Both carrying capacity and LAC have direct implications for Iran's heritage forests. For example, the Hyrcanian Forests receive large numbers of domestic tourists during holidays, often leading to overcrowding, waste accumulation, and habitat disturbance. Applying LAC frameworks could help identify thresholds for trail erosion, wildlife disturbance, or cultural disruption, guiding the design of visitor management strategies. Similarly, carrying capacity assessments could inform infrastructure development, ensuring that roads, picnic areas, and campsites do not exceed the ecological resilience of forest ecosystems. By integrating these tools into national tourism planning, Iran could move toward a more balanced approach that reconciles visitor demand with long-term conservation goals (Aktymbayeva et al., 2023).

1.6 Environmental Ethics and Tourism

1.6.1 Anthropocentric vs. Eco-friendly Perspectives

Environmental ethics provides the philosophical foundation for understanding how societies conceptualize their relationship with nature. The dominant paradigm for centuries has been anthropocentrism, which views the environment primarily in terms of its utility for human beings. In this view, forests, rivers, and landscapes are valuable insofar as they provide resources, economic benefits, or aesthetic enjoyment. Tourism has largely reflected this orientation: destinations are marketed as commodities for human consumption, and natural resources are developed to maximize visitor satisfaction. This perspective has enabled rapid tourism growth but has also led to overexploitation and environmental degradation (Nathaniel & Adedoyin, 2022).

In contrast, Eco-friendly perspectives argue that nature possesses intrinsic value independent of human use. From this standpoint, forests and ecosystems are not merely resources but living systems with their own rights to exist and regenerate. This ethical position has gained traction in environmental philosophy and conservation movements, especially in light of biodiversity loss and climate change. Ecocentrism calls for a radical rethinking of tourism: rather than treating natural landscapes as backdrops for human enjoyment, tourism should be restructured around respect for ecological integrity and long-term sustainability (Baloch et al., 2023).

The tension between anthropocentrism and ecocentrism plays out vividly in tourism contexts. For example, mass tourism in sensitive ecosystems often reflects anthropocentric priorities, privileging short-term economic gains over ecological stability. By contrast, community-based ecotourism or spiritual tourism initiatives often embody more Eco-friendly values, emphasizing harmony with nature, low-impact activities, and respect for local traditions. For Iran, where cultural and religious traditions often highlight stewardship of the natural world, Eco-friendly perspectives could serve as a bridge between global sustainability debates and local ethical frameworks (Bieling et al., 2020).

1.6.2 Rights of Nature: Conceptual Origins and Global Adoption

One of the most significant developments in environmental ethics is the emergence of the Rights of Nature (RoN) movement. Rooted in indigenous cosmologies and Eco-friendly philosophy, RoN challenges the assumption that nature is merely property or a resource. Instead, it proposes that ecosystems and species have legal rights to exist, thrive, and regenerate. This shift mirrors the expansion of rights historically granted to marginalized groups, extending moral and legal recognition to non-human entities (Petersmann, 2024).

RoN has moved beyond theoretical discourse into practical legal frameworks. Ecuador's 2008 Constitution was the first to explicitly enshrine the Rights of Nature, recognizing Pachamama (Mother Earth) as a rights-bearing entity. Bolivia followed with the "Law of the Rights of Mother Earth" in 2010, framing nature as a subject of legal protection. New Zealand has pioneered case-specific applications by granting legal personhood to the Whanganui River and The Urewera Forest, recognizing indigenous Māori traditions that see these landscapes as ancestors. These examples have inspired similar initiatives in Colombia, India, and the United States, signaling a growing global movement toward Eco-friendly governance.

The adoption of RoN has profound implications for tourism. By recognizing ecosystems as rights-bearing entities, tourism development must respect ecological thresholds and prioritize conservation over commodification. This legal innovation reframes the debate: instead of asking how many tourists a site can host, managers must ask whether tourism activities infringe upon the rights of the ecosystem itself. Such a framework could transform heritage forest tourism in Iran by shifting the focus from maximizing visitor numbers to safeguarding ecological integrity as a fundamental right (Ghorbani et al., 2023).

1.6.3 The Moral Duty to Protect Heritage Forests

Beyond legal frameworks, environmental ethics emphasizes the moral responsibility of societies to protect heritage forests as shared legacies of humanity. The concept of intergenerational justice is central here: current generations have an obligation to safeguard ecosystems not only for their own benefit but also for future generations. Forests are irreplaceable ecological systems that take centuries to evolve; their destruction represents not only a loss for present communities but also a deprivation of opportunities for those yet to come. Tourism, when poorly managed, threatens to undermine this duty by prioritizing short-term economic gains over long-term ecological health (Smith et al., 2023).

The moral duty to protect forests also extends to respecting cultural traditions that view them as sacred or spiritually significant. In many societies, including Iran, forests are embedded in cultural practices, festivals, and local beliefs. This cultural dimension reinforces the ethical argument for protection: to destroy forests is not merely an ecological loss but also an erosion of cultural identity and continuity. By recognizing the cultural and spiritual values of forests, tourism planning can align with ethical frameworks that go beyond economic calculations (Constant & Taylor, 2020).

For Iran, adopting an ethical approach to forest tourism could strengthen both conservation and cultural resilience. The Hyrcanian and Zagros forests are not only ecological treasures but also living symbols of national heritage. Protecting them requires acknowledging their intrinsic rights and recognizing the moral duty of stewardship. Tourism can play a positive role if it is designed as an instrument of environmental education and cultural respect, fostering awareness among visitors of their ethical responsibilities. In this way, environmental ethics provides both a philosophical foundation and a practical guide for rethinking the future of heritage forest tourism in Iran (Tauro et al., 2021).

1.7 Linking Tourism, Heritage, and Nature Rights

1.7.1 Conceptual Overlaps and Tensions

Tourism, heritage, and nature rights are interconnected concepts, yet their interaction is often marked by tension. Tourism depends on natural and cultural heritage for its very existence, drawing visitors to unique landscapes, forests, monuments, and traditions. Heritage, in turn, benefits from tourism through increased visibility, international recognition, and revenue that can support conservation. The Rights of Nature framework deepens this relationship by affirming that ecosystems have intrinsic value and deserve protection regardless of their utility for tourism or human enjoyment. At first glance, these three spheres appear complementary, pointing toward a model where tourism fosters heritage appreciation while respecting nature's rights (Z. Zhang et al., 2023).

However, tensions quickly emerge when these spheres are placed into practice. Tourism frequently commodifies heritage, reducing forests or rituals to marketable attractions. While this may generate short-term economic benefits, it can undermine both ecological resilience and cultural authenticity. Heritage management frameworks such as UNESCO emphasize conservation, but inscription often leads to mass visitation, which contradicts the very goal of preservation. Similarly, the Rights of Nature challenges anthropocentric tourism models, demanding limits on exploitation that may conflict with the economic priorities of states and private enterprises. Thus, the overlap between tourism, heritage, and nature rights is as much a contradiction as it is of complementarity.

The key challenge lies in reconciling these tensions through governance frameworks that integrate the principles of sustainability, heritage conservation, and eco-friendly ethics. Doing so requires a fundamental shift in how societies conceptualize the purpose of tourism. Instead of viewing tourism primarily as an engine of growth, it must be reframed as a practice of stewardship and education, one that respects both heritage values and the intrinsic rights of nature (Liburd et al., 2024).

1.7.2 The Conservation–Commodification Paradox

The paradox of conservation and commodification is central to debates about tourism and heritage. On one side, tourism generates financial resources that can be reinvested into conservation projects, infrastructure, and community development. On the other side, the commercialization of heritage often reduces it to a product for consumption, stripping away deeper meanings and threatening ecological integrity. This paradox is particularly visible in forest ecosystems, where heritage designation may increase protection in law while simultaneously inviting unsustainable levels of visitation in practice (Youdelis et al., 2020).

Globally, examples abound. Machu Picchu in Peru attracts millions of visitors annually, generating substantial revenue for conservation and national identity. Yet, overcrowding has led to erosion, waste accumulation, and pressures on local communities. Venice faces similar contradictions: the city's heritage attracts tourists who contribute economically but overwhelm its infrastructure and displace residents. Iran's Hyrcanian Forests reflect the same paradox. Inscription as a UNESCO World Heritage Site in 2019 raised global awareness and national pride but also intensified domestic tourism, leading to increased waste and ecological stress. These cases reveal how heritage recognition can inadvertently accelerate commodification (Tehseen et al., 2024).

Addressing this paradox requires shifting from quantity-driven to quality-driven tourism models. Concepts such as "slow tourism," "community-based tourism," and "high-value, low-impact tourism" offer pathways toward reconciling conservation with economic viability. The Rights of Nature framework adds a critical dimension by insisting that ecosystems themselves must not be commodified beyond their ecological thresholds. For Iran, adopting such frameworks could help ensure that tourism supports conservation rather than undermining it, aligning heritage protection with broader ethical obligations (Mandić et al., 2025).

1.7.3 Toward an Integrated Framework

The integration of tourism, heritage, and nature rights requires moving beyond fragmented approaches toward a holistic model. Such a framework would recognize that tourism cannot be separated from the ecological systems and cultural landscapes it depends upon. It would treat forests not as mere tourist destinations but as heritage entities with intrinsic rights and long-term value. This requires combining the strengths of existing global frameworks UNESCO's heritage recognition, IUCN's scientific conservation tools, and GSTC's tourism standards with the ethical innovations of the Rights of Nature movement (Paing et al., 2022).

An integrated framework would operate on three levels. First, at the policy level, governments must align tourism development with conservation goals, embedding environmental ethics into national planning. Second, at the community level, local stakeholders must be empowered to participate in decision-making, ensuring that heritage is protected not only for tourists but also for those who depend on it culturally and economically. Third, at the educational level, tourism must be reimagined as a vehicle for raising awareness of ecological limits and ethical responsibilities, rather than as mere entertainment. Such a framework shifts the focus from profit maximization to stewardship, aligning economic, cultural, and ecological priorities (Skrimizea & Parra, 2019).

For Iran, this integrated approach holds particular promise. Heritage forests such as the Hyrcanian and Zagros ecosystems are ecological treasures, cultural legacies, and tourism destinations all at once. Managing them requires policies that reconcile these overlapping dimensions rather than treating them in isolation. By adopting an integrated framework, Iran could position itself as a leader in sustainable heritage tourism, demonstrating how tourism can serve as a bridge between conservation, cultural identity, and ecological ethics. This vision provides a pathway for addressing current challenges while laying the foundation for a more sustainable and respectful tourism future (Jong, 2024).

1.8 Relevance for Iran and Heritage Forests

The conceptual debates surrounding tourism, environment, and heritage acquire particular urgency in the Iranian context. Iran is home to two major forest ecosystems of global significance: the Hyrcanian Forests along the Caspian Sea and the Zagros Forests in western Iran. These forests are not only ecological treasures harboring unique species, regulating climate, and storing carbon but also cultural landscapes deeply embedded in Iranian identity. Their inscription on the UNESCO World Heritage List, particularly the Hyrcanian Forests in 2019, situates Iran within international heritage discourses and highlights the global importance of their preservation. However, recognition also brings heightened tourism pressures, raising questions about how to reconcile heritage protection with economic development and visitor demand (Jagielska-Burduk et al., 2021).

Tourism in Iran's forests is primarily domestic, with millions of visitors flocking to natural areas during public holidays and weekends. While this reflects the cultural importance of forests as recreational spaces, it also generates significant environmental pressures. Waste accumulation, off-road driving, illegal logging, and habitat disturbance are persistent challenges. Inadequate infrastructure such as waste disposal facilities, eco-friendly accommodations, and visitor education programs exacerbates these problems. Without careful management, tourism risks accelerating the degradation of forests that are already vulnerable to deforestation, overgrazing, and climate change (Madani et al., 2024).

The Rights of Nature framework offers an innovative lens through which to reconsider forest tourism in Iran. While Iranian law does not formally recognize ecosystems as rights-bearing entities, cultural and religious traditions emphasize stewardship of the natural world. Concepts from Islamic environmental ethics, such as Amanat (trusteeship) and Khalifa (stewardship), resonate with the eco-friendly values promoted by RoN. Applying these principles to tourism could help reframe forests not simply as resources for human enjoyment but as living heritage with intrinsic rights. By integrating international frameworks (UNESCO, IUCN, GSTC) with indigenous values and RoN ethics, Iran can craft a unique model of sustainable heritage tourism (Ghorbani et al., 2023).

Ultimately, the relevance of these debates for Iran lies in their practical implications. Heritage forests must be protected not only for their ecological value but also for their role in national identity, cultural continuity, and international reputation. Tourism, if carefully managed, can contribute to this protection by generating revenue, raising awareness, and strengthening community engagement. However, if mismanaged, it risks undermining both ecological resilience and cultural integrity. The task for Iranian policymakers, scholars, and communities is therefore to navigate these tensions, creating a model of tourism that honors both heritage values and the rights of nature (Hariram et al., 2023).

1.9 Conclusion

This chapter has established the conceptual foundation for understanding the complex relationships between tourism, environment, heritage, and the emerging discourse of nature rights. It began by situating tourism within global economic and cultural systems, highlighting its dependence on ecological integrity and heritage values. It then explored the evolution of heritage as a concept, recognizing forests as living cultural landscapes that embody both ecological and cultural significance. The paradox of tourism offering both conservation opportunities and risks of commodification was analyzed alongside global frameworks such as UNESCO, IUCN, and the GSTC. Environmental ethics, particularly the distinction between anthropocentric and Eco-friendly perspectives, provided a philosophical lens for rethinking tourism's role in heritage management.

The chapter also emphasized the transformative potential of the Rights of Nature framework. By granting ecosystems intrinsic rights, RoN challenges conventional tourism models and demands a shift toward stewardship and respect for ecological thresholds. Although not yet formally adopted in Iran, the framework resonates with cultural and religious traditions that emphasize care for the natural world. When combined with international frameworks and community-based strategies, RoN can offer a pathway toward more ethical and sustainable tourism practices.

For Iran, these conceptual debates are far from abstract. Heritage forests such as the Hyrcanian and Zagros ecosystems are at the center of national identity, ecological resilience, and tourism development. Their protection is critical not only for Iran's cultural and environmental future but also for its engagement with global heritage discourses. Tourism presents both risks and opportunities: it can either accelerate ecological degradation or serve as a powerful tool for conservation and education. The direction taken will depend on the frameworks adopted, the policies implemented, and the values embraced.

Looking ahead, this chapter sets the stage for the rest of the book. Chapter 2 will focus specifically on Iran's forest ecosystems and cultural heritage, examining their ecological importance and historical significance. By grounding the discussion in both global frameworks and local realities, the analysis will provide a comprehensive basis for understanding how Iran can move toward a model of sustainable heritage tourism that respects both human needs and the intrinsic rights of nature.

CHAPTER 2

FOREST ECOSYSTEMS AND CULTURAL HERITAGE IN IRAN

2.1 Introduction

Forests in Iran represent some of the most significant ecological and cultural landscapes in the Middle East and Central Asia. Although forested land constitutes less than 10 percent of the country's total area, these ecosystems play a disproportionately important role in maintaining biodiversity, regulating climate, and supporting human livelihoods. From the lush Hyrcanian forests along the Caspian Sea to the rugged oak woodlands of the Zagros Mountains, Iran's forests embody a diversity of ecological conditions shaped by geography, climate, and history. Beyond their environmental functions, these forests are also deeply embedded in cultural narratives, shaping collective memory, religious symbolism, and local traditions. They are, in short, not only ecological resources but also cultural heritage (Jagielska-Burduk et al., 2021).

In global terms, Iran's forests occupy a distinctive position. The Hyrcanian Forests, inscribed on the UNESCO World Heritage List in 2019, are considered living relics of the Tertiary period, hosting unique flora and fauna that have survived millions of years of climatic shifts. The Zagros Forests, stretching across western Iran, form one of the world's largest oak-dominated ecosystems and are intimately linked to the nomadic pastoralist traditions that have defined Iranian rural life for centuries. Lesser-known ecosystems such as the Arasbaran forests in the northwest and mangroves in the Persian Gulf further enrich the country's ecological diversity, highlighting Iran's importance as a custodian of unique and varied forest environments (Mehri et al., 2024).

At the same time, Iran's forests are under increasing pressure from both anthropogenic and natural factors. Rapid urbanization, agricultural expansion, overgrazing, and illegal logging have contributed to deforestation and habitat fragmentation. Climate change adds another layer of vulnerability, intensifying droughts, pest outbreaks, and forest fires. Tourism, though potentially a vehicle for conservation, often exacerbates these pressures due to unregulated visitation, inadequate waste management, and infrastructural shortcomings. This dual role of tourism as both a threat and an opportunity raises urgent questions about how Iran can balance ecological conservation with heritage appreciation and sustainable development (Ghaderi & Henderson, 2012).

This chapter explores the ecological and cultural significance of Iran's forests within the broader framework of heritage and tourism. It begins with a detailed examination of the Hyrcanian and Zagros forests as the country's two dominant forest systems, followed by an overview of lesser-known ecosystems. The chapter then highlights the biodiversity and ecosystem services of Iranian forests, situating them within global environmental debates. It also examines forests as cultural and spiritual heritage, emphasizing their role in literature, mythology, and traditional practices. Finally, the chapter addresses the challenges posed by tourism, deforestation, and governance gaps, while underscoring the urgent need to reimagine forests as living heritage that must be safeguarded for both present and future generations (Rollo, 2025).

2.2 The Hyrcanian Forests: An Ancient World Heritage Ecosystem

2.2.1 Geological and Ecological History

The Hyrcanian Forests, stretching along the southern shores of the Caspian Sea and covering five northern provinces of Iran, represent one of the oldest surviving broadleaf forests in the world. Geologically, these forests are remnants of the Tertiary period, dating back between 25 and 50 million years. At a time when much of Europe and parts of Asia experienced extensive glaciation, the Hyrcanian region remained climatically stable, providing a refuge for species that disappeared elsewhere. This unique history explains why the forests are often described as "living fossils," preserving ancient lineages of flora that have vanished from other parts of the planet. Their survival across multiple geological epochs makes them a critical site for understanding both ecological resilience and evolutionary continuity (Markley et al., 2025).

Ecologically, the Hyrcanian Forests are dominated by broadleaf deciduous trees, with species composition varying according to altitude, soil type, and microclimate. The lower elevations are characterized by mixed deciduous stands of hornbeam (Carpinus betulus), beech (Fagus orientalis), and alder (Alnus subcordata), while higher elevations are dominated by beech forests. In total, the Hyrcanian region hosts more than 3,200 vascular plant species, including many endemics that are found nowhere else. This botanical richness is the product of both the forests' ancient origins and their role as ecological refugia during climatic fluctuations. The region thus provides scientists with a natural laboratory for studying speciation, adaptation, and long-term ecological processes (Ernst et al., 2025).

The ecological importance of the Hyrcanian Forests extends beyond their flora. Their structure and microclimates provide habitat for a diverse array of fauna, including large mammals such as the Persian leopard (Panthera pardus saxicolor), brown bear (Ursus arctos), and wild boar (Sus scrofa), as well as numerous bird, reptile, and amphibian species. Many of these species are threatened or endangered, underscoring the global conservation value of the Hyrcanian ecosystem. The ecological continuity of the forests also contributes to broader environmental stability: they regulate regional hydrological cycles, protect soil from erosion, and act as carbon sinks. In this sense, their geological and ecological history is directly linked to contemporary debates about climate change and biodiversity loss (Flood et al., 2025).

The forests' ancient pedigree also shapes their symbolic and cultural significance. As ecosystems that have survived for millions of years, the Hyrcanian Forests evoke ideas of endurance, continuity, and resilience. This perception has been reinforced by their inscription as a UNESCO World Heritage Site in 2019, which formally recognized both their geological antiquity and their ecological uniqueness. For Iran, the Hyrcanian Forests serve as a reminder of its role as a custodian of one of the world's most ancient ecosystems. Preserving them is therefore not only a matter of national pride but also an international responsibility, ensuring that this irreplaceable relic of Earth's natural history continues to survive for future generations (Sengar & Shah, 2025).

2.2.2 Flora and Fauna Diversity

The Hyrcanian Forests are globally renowned for their extraordinary botanical richness, hosting over 3,200 vascular plant species, of which nearly 400 are endemic. This high degree of endemism reflects the forests' role as ecological refugia during the Ice Ages, when many European species were wiped out but survived in the relatively stable Caspian climatic zone. The forests are dominated by broadleaf deciduous trees, with Oriental beech (Fagus orientalis) serving as the keystone species at higher elevations. Other characteristic trees include hornbeam (Carpinus betulus), chestnut-leaved oak (Quercus castaneifolia), ironwood (Parrotia persica), and alder (Alnus subcordata). The presence of the ironwood tree, which is endemic to the Hyrcanian region, highlights the unique evolutionary history of these forests and their importance as a "living museum" of ancient flora (Nielsen, 2025).

The understory vegetation is highly diverse, comprising shrubs, ferns, mosses, and wildflowers that flourish in the humid microclimates formed beneath the dense canopy cover. Species such as the Hyrcanian boxwood (Buxus hyrcana) and a variety of medicinal plants contribute to the forests' ecological and cultural value. For centuries, local communities have relied on these plants for traditional medicine, weaving, and artisanal products, linking biodiversity directly to cultural practices. Seasonal variations also enhance floral diversity: spring carpets of anemones and wild tulips, summer foliage, and autumnal colors contribute to the forests' aesthetic appeal, making them major attractions for nature tourism (Yang et al., 2023).

In terms of fauna, the Hyrcanian Forests serve as critical habitats for numerous species, including several large carnivores that are emblematic of Iran's wildlife heritage. The Persian leopard (Panthera pardus saxicolor), one of the largest leopard subspecies, is the most iconic and endangered species in the region. Other notable mammals include the brown bear (Ursus arctos), lynx (Lynx lynx), wild cat (Felis silvestris), and wild boar (Sus scrofa). The forests are also home to deer species such as the red deer (Cervus elaphus) and roe deer (Capreolus capreolus), as well as smaller mammals like hedgehogs, squirrels, and foxes. The presence of these species underscores the forests' role as biodiversity hotspots, although many populations face threats from habitat loss, poaching, and human–wildlife conflict (Shokri et al., 2021).

Avifauna further enriches the Hyrcanian ecosystem. The region is a key migratory corridor for birds traveling between Siberia and Africa, supporting over 300 bird species, including raptors, waterfowl, and songbirds. Endangered species such as the white-headed duck (Oxyura leucocephala) and the imperial eagle (Aquila heliaca) rely on the forests and surrounding wetlands for nesting and feeding. Amphibians and reptiles, including the endangered Caspian turtle (Mauremys caspica), also inhabit the area, highlighting the ecological diversity across multiple taxa. Collectively, the flora and fauna of the Hyrcanian Forests make them one of the most biologically significant temperate forests in the world, reinforcing their recognition as a UNESCO World Heritage Site and emphasizing the need for stronger conservation measures (Sohrabi, 2025).

2.2.3 UNESCO World Heritage Designation (2019)

The inscription of the Hyrcanian Forests on the UNESCO World Heritage List in July 2019 marked a significant milestone for Iran's environmental and cultural diplomacy. Recognized under natural criteria (ix) and (x) of the World Heritage Convention, the forests were acknowledged for their outstanding universal value as living relics of the Tertiary period and as critical habitats for biodiversity conservation. This designation placed the Hyrcanian Forests among the most ecologically significant temperate forests in the world, aligning Iran with global conservation priorities and reinforcing the country's role as a custodian of ancient ecosystems. For UNESCO, the forests exemplify evolutionary processes and ecological resilience across millions of years, making them irreplaceable from both scientific and cultural perspectives (Fairclough, 2019).

The process of inscription was the culmination of years of national and international advocacy. Iranian researchers, conservationists, and policymakers collaborated to prepare the nomination dossier, supported by scientific evaluations from the International Union for Conservation of Nature (IUCN). The recognition of the forests' exceptional biodiversity—over 3,200 plant species, several large mammal populations, and important bird habitats—strengthened the case for inscription. In addition, the forests' role as refugia during the Ice Ages, which enabled the survival of plant lineages extinct elsewhere, underscored their uniqueness at the global scale. UNESCO's designation thus affirmed that the Hyrcanian Forests are not only of national importance but also of universal significance (Trajkovska Petkoska et al., 2025).

For Iran, World Heritage recognition carries both opportunities and responsibilities. On one hand, it enhances the country's international visibility, attracting tourists, researchers, and conservation funding. It also strengthens Iran's environmental diplomacy, positioning the country as a partner in global sustainability initiatives. On the other hand, inscription imposes obligations: Iran is required to maintain the ecological integrity of the forests, submit periodic conservation reports, and implement management strategies aligned with UNESCO guidelines. Failure to meet these standards could lead to the forests being placed on the "World Heritage in Danger" list, which would undermine both their international standing and Iran's reputation in conservation governance (Shokri et al., 2021).

The UNESCO designation also highlights the paradox of recognition. While global visibility can promote conservation, it can also fuel mass tourism that threatens the very resources meant to be protected. Since 2019, the Hyrcanian Forests have experienced a surge in domestic tourism, particularly during national holidays, creating new pressures such as waste accumulation, habitat disturbance, and infrastructural strain. This dynamic illustrates the double-edged nature of heritage recognition: while it elevates the symbolic and diplomatic importance of the forests, it also increases their vulnerability. Managing this tension requires Iran to balance international obligations with domestic realities, integrating sustainable tourism practices and community-based conservation into the broader management framework (Ghaderi & Henderson, 2012).

2.2.4 Cultural and Historical Significance

The Hyrcanian Forests are not only ecological treasures but also cultural landscapes that have shaped Iranian identity for millennia. References to these forests appear in Persian mythology, epic poetry, and historical chronicles, where they are often portrayed as spaces of mystery, abundance, and resilience.

In the Shahnameh (Book of Kings) by Ferdowsi, forests of the Caspian region are depicted as settings for legendary battles and heroic quests, symbolizing both natural wealth and formidable wilderness. Such representations highlight the forests as more than physical environments: they are symbolic spaces woven into the cultural memory of Iran. These literary depictions continue to influence how Iranians perceive their natural heritage, reinforcing the idea that forests embody both beauty and strength (Abouei & Tavasoli, 2024).

Persian poetry and literature more broadly have celebrated forests as metaphors for spiritual renewal, love, and endurance. Poets such as Hafez and Saadi used natural imagery trees, shade, and woodland paths to evoke moral and spiritual lessons. Although not always referring directly to the Hyrcanian Forests, these symbolic uses of forest imagery reflect a broader cultural valuation of wooded landscapes in Iranian thought. The forests are also prominent in visual arts and miniature paintings, where they appear as backgrounds for courtly life or spiritual contemplation. In this sense, the Hyrcanian woodlands are cultural symbols that transcend their ecological boundaries, serving as metaphors for harmony, wisdom, and the continuity of life (Olivadese, 2025).

At the local level, the Hyrcanian Forests have long shaped the livelihoods and traditions of surrounding communities. Villages within and adjacent to the forests have historically depended on them for fuelwood, medicinal plants, and construction materials, while also developing knowledge systems that ensure sustainable use. Traditional practices such as seasonal grazing, gathering of non-timber products, and small-scale agriculture reflect centuries of coexistence with forest ecosystems. Rituals tied to seasonal cycles—such as spring festivals linked to Nowruz often involve forest landscapes as spaces of community gathering, renewal, and celebration. These practices demonstrate how the forests are embedded not only in national culture but also in the everyday lives of local people (Tseer et al., 2025).

The spiritual dimension of the Hyrcanian Forests is equally significant. Certain groves and trees are considered sacred, associated with local saints or believed to harbor protective spirits. These sacred sites are visited for blessings, healing, or prayer, reflecting an enduring belief in the forests as spaces of spiritual power. Such traditions echo broader patterns across Iran, where natural elements mountains, rivers, and trees are imbued with symbolic meaning. By serving as sites of both religious practice and cultural identity, the Hyrcanian Forests embody the concept of living heritage, where natural and cultural values are inseparably intertwined. Recognizing this dual significance is essential for developing tourism strategies that respect not only ecological integrity but also the cultural meanings that make the forests unique (Nathaniel & Adedoyin, 2022).

2.2.5 Tourism in the Hyrcanian Forests

Tourism in the Hyrcanian Forests has grown significantly in recent decades, driven by both domestic demand and the forests' increasing international recognition. The region's lush landscapes, diverse wildlife, and unique microclimates offer a striking contrast to Iran's arid and semi-arid environments, making the forests especially attractive to visitors seeking recreation and relief. Popular destinations within the Hyrcanian belt include the provinces of Gilan, Mazandaran, and Golestan, where tourists enjoy hiking, camping, picnicking, and exploring waterfalls and mountain trails. Seasonal changes add to the forests' appeal: spring wildflowers, autumn foliage, and winter snowfall each provide distinct experiences, reinforcing the forests' reputation as year-round tourism destinations (Sohrabi, 2025).

Beyond recreation, the Hyrcanian Forests have considerable potential for ecotourism development. Their designation as a UNESCO World Heritage Site has raised their international profile, creating opportunities for eco-lodges, guided wildlife tours, and educational programs that highlight biodiversity and cultural traditions. Ecotourism could generate alternative livelihoods for local communities, reducing reliance on extractive practices such as logging or overgrazing. Successful examples from other countries, such as Costa Rica or Nepal, suggest that with careful planning, ecotourism can both strengthen conservation efforts and provide stable income streams. For Iran, promoting ecotourism in the Hyrcanian region could diversify its tourism industry, which is often focused on cultural and historical attractions, and help position the country as a leader in sustainable forest-based tourism (Zahed et al., 2022).

Despite this potential, the reality of tourism in the Hyrcanian Forests is often characterized by mass domestic visitation with limited regulation. During holidays and weekends, thousands of visitors travel to the forests, often without adequate infrastructure for waste disposal, parking, or camping facilities. This results in widespread littering, soil compaction, and disturbance of wildlife habitats. Informal picnicking, a deeply rooted cultural practice, creates additional pressures, as food waste and single-use plastics accumulate in sensitive areas. Off-road vehicles and unregulated construction of resorts or villas within forest zones further exacerbate degradation. These issues highlight the gap between the forests' symbolic recognition as heritage sites and the practical challenges of managing tourism sustainably (Tehseen et al., 2024).

The key challenge is to balance tourism development with ecological and cultural integrity. Achieving this requires coordinated policies that integrate international sustainability standards, national tourism strategies, and local community participation. Visitor education campaigns, stricter enforcement of environmental regulations, and investment in eco-friendly infrastructure are critical first steps. At the same time, tourism must be reframed not as a threat but as a potential tool for conservation, capable of generating funds and public support for protecting the Hyrcanian Forests. By moving from unregulated mass visitation to carefully managed ecotourism, Iran could transform the forests into models of sustainable heritage tourism, where ecological preservation, cultural traditions, and visitor enjoyment coexist in harmony (Sharma, 2025).

2.2.6 Threats and Conservation Challenges

The Hyrcanian Forests, despite their global significance and UNESCO designation, face a wide range of threats that jeopardize their long-term survival. One of the most pressing challenges is deforestation and habitat fragmentation driven by human activities. Agricultural expansion, particularly the conversion of forest land into rice paddies, orchards, and tea plantations in the Caspian provinces, continues to erode forest cover. Illegal logging for timber and fuelwood further compounds the problem, leading to biodiversity loss and soil degradation. Expanding road networks and unplanned urbanization fragment habitats, disrupting wildlife corridors and reducing the ecological resilience of the forests. These pressures are intensified by population growth and the rising demand for land and resources in northern Iran (Leal Filho et al., 2023).

Another major challenge is climate change, which threatens to alter the ecological balance of the Hyrcanian Forests. Rising temperatures, prolonged droughts, and irregular precipitation patterns have increased the frequency and severity of wildfires in recent years. Pest outbreaks, such as those caused by bark beetles, are also becoming more frequent, weakening tree populations and accelerating forest decline. Climate change not only affects the forests directly but also amplifies other threats, such as water scarcity and agricultural expansion, creating a vicious cycle of ecological stress. Given that the Hyrcanian Forests have survived multiple climatic epochs over millions of years, their vulnerability to modern climate change underscores the severity of current anthropogenic pressures (Page & Connell, 2020).

Tourism, while a potential tool for conservation, also poses serious management challenges when unregulated. The surge of domestic tourism following the forests' UNESCO recognition has led to uncontrolled visitation, waste accumulation, and habitat disturbance. Picnic culture, off-road driving, and unplanned construction of tourist facilities have created localized but severe ecological damage. Moreover, the absence of systematic monitoring and enforcement has allowed these practices to persist unchecked. Without proper infrastructure such as designated trails, waste management systems, and eco-friendly accommodations tourism risks accelerating degradation rather than supporting conservation. This illustrates the paradox of heritage recognition: global visibility can attract conservation funding but also amplify local pressures (Scheyvens & van der Watt, 2021).

Finally, the Hyrcanian Forests suffer from weak governance and fragmented policy frameworks. Although multiple agencies including the Iranian Department of Environment, the Forests, Range and Watershed Management Organization, and local municipalities are involved in management, overlapping mandates and limited coordination hinder effective action. Corruption, insufficient funding, and inadequate enforcement of environmental regulations further undermine conservation efforts. Community participation in forest management is also limited, even though local populations have historically served as custodians of these landscapes. Addressing these governance gaps is crucial: without integrated policies and strong enforcement mechanisms, conservation strategies will remain ineffective. The challenge is therefore not only ecological but also institutional, requiring reforms that align local, national, and international efforts to safeguard the Hyrcanian Forests (Niknam et al., 2024).

2.2.7 Toward Sustainable Management

The future of the Hyrcanian Forests depends on developing effective strategies that balance ecological protection, cultural heritage, and tourism development. Iran has established a series of legal and institutional frameworks for forest management, including the Forests, Range, and Watershed Management Organization (FRWO) and the Department of Environment. These bodies are tasked with monitoring forest use, preventing illegal logging, and coordinating conservation programs. However, enforcement remains inconsistent, and management strategies often lack a long-term vision. To move toward sustainable management, national policies must shift from a focus on resource exploitation to one of ecological stewardship, integrating conservation goals into broader economic and development planning (Madani et al., 2024).

One promising pathway is the implementation of community-based forest management (CBFM) models. Local communities have historically served as custodians of the Hyrcanian Forests, relying on them for livelihoods while maintaining cultural traditions of stewardship. Revitalizing these practices through participatory governance could strengthen conservation while also ensuring equitable benefits from tourism. Examples from Nepal and Mexico demonstrate that when communities are given legal rights to manage forests, biodiversity outcomes improve, and deforestation rates decline. For Iran, adapting such models would require legal reforms, capacity building, and mechanisms for equitable revenue-sharing from forest tourism and ecotourism initiatives (Cheer et al., 2019).

Another dimension of sustainable management involves aligning with international frameworks and best practices. UNESCO's guidelines for World Heritage Sites emphasize the need for comprehensive management plans, visitor impact monitoring, and stakeholder engagement. Similarly, IUCN offers scientific standards for ecosystem management, while the Global Sustainable Tourism Council (GSTC) provides practical criteria for sustainable tourism development. By adopting these frameworks, Iran can harmonize its national policies with international expectations, ensuring that conservation efforts meet both domestic needs and global obligations. Integration of these standards could also enhance Iran's access to international funding and technical expertise, strengthening its capacity to manage the forests effectively (Nielsen, 2025).

The concept of the Rights of Nature (RoN) provides an innovative normative framework that could reshape forest governance in Iran. Although not formally recognized in Iranian law, RoN resonates with cultural and religious traditions emphasizing stewardship (amanat) and trusteeship (khalifa) of the natural world. Recognizing the Hyrcanian Forests as entities with intrinsic rights to exist and regenerate would fundamentally shift the ethical foundation of forest management. Under such a framework, tourism and development activities would need to be assessed not only in terms of human benefit but also in terms of their impact on the forests' rights. This perspective could help Iran move beyond reactive conservation measures toward a proactive ethic of ecological respect (Leal Filho et al., 2023).

Finally, sustainable management requires educational and cultural initiatives that reframe public attitudes toward forests. Environmental education programs, eco-tourism campaigns, and cultural festivals celebrating the Hyrcanian Forests could foster greater awareness among visitors and local residents alike. By cultivating a culture of respect and stewardship, such initiatives would complement institutional reforms and international standards. In this way, sustainable management becomes not merely a technical exercise but a holistic strategy that integrates policy, community participation, global frameworks, ethical principles, and cultural education. For Iran, adopting such a comprehensive approach could transform the Hyrcanian Forests into a global model of how ancient ecosystems can be preserved as living heritage in the twenty-first century (N. Khan et al., 2020).

2.3 The Zagros Forests: Cultural Landscapes of Pastoralism

2.3.1 Introduction to the Zagros Forests

The Zagros Forests form one of the most extensive and ecologically significant ecosystems in Iran, stretching across the western and southwestern parts of the country. Covering approximately five million hectares nearly 40 percent of Iran's total forest area the Zagros region spans over ten provinces, including Kurdistan, Kermanshah, Lorestan, Chaharmahal and Bakhtiari, and Khuzestan. Geographically, the forests are distributed along the Zagros mountain range, which extends from northwestern Iran down to the Persian Gulf. The sheer scale of these forests makes them vital not only for Iran's biodiversity but also for regional ecological stability, as they regulate water cycles, protect soils from erosion, and provide resources for millions of people (Sadeghi & Hazbavi, 2022).

Ecologically, the Zagros Forests are characterized primarily by oak-dominated woodlands, particularly the Persian oak (Quercus brantii), which accounts for more than half of the forest cover. These oak forests are interspersed with pistachio (Pistacia atlantica), wild almond (Amygdalus scoparia), and other drought-resistant species adapted to the semi-arid conditions of the Zagros Mountains. Despite their relative simplicity in species composition compared to the Hyrcanian Forests, the Zagros woodlands support a wide range of wildlife, including wild goats, gazelles, wolves, and a variety of bird species. Their ecological functions extend beyond biodiversity: they act as watersheds feeding major rivers such as the Karun and Karkheh, which are critical for agriculture and human settlements in western and southern Iran (Shahraki et al., 2023).

Beyond their ecological importance, the Zagros Forests are deeply embedded in the cultural fabric of Iran. For centuries, they have sustained nomadic and semi-nomadic pastoralist communities, including the Bakhtiari, Qashqai, and Kurdish tribes. These groups have developed intricate systems of seasonal migration (transhumance), moving livestock between lowland winter pastures and highland summer meadows. The forests provide fodder, fuelwood, and shelter, while also serving as symbolic landscapes in tribal folklore, rituals, and oral traditions. Thus, the Zagros are not simply natural ecosystems but cultural landscapes, shaped by millennia of human–environment interactions (Farina, 2022).

Despite their significance, the Zagros Forests face mounting pressures that threaten their ecological integrity and cultural continuity. Deforestation, overgrazing, and land conversion for agriculture have severely reduced forest cover, while climate change exacerbates drought and desertification in the region. At the same time, the erosion of pastoralist traditions under modernization has weakened traditional stewardship practices, leaving forests more vulnerable to unsustainable exploitation. These challenges underscore the urgency of developing strategies that recognize the Zagros as both ecological and cultural heritage. This section therefore examines the ecological characteristics, cultural significance, tourism potential, and conservation challenges of the Zagros Forests, highlighting their role as living landscapes at the intersection of nature and culture (Khosravi Mashizi & Sharafatmandrad, 2023).

2.3.2 Ecological Characteristics

The Zagros Forests are dominated by oak woodlands, which form the backbone of the ecosystem. The most prominent species is the Persian oak (Quercus brantii), covering nearly 70 percent of the forest area. This oak is well adapted to the semi-arid climate of western Iran, thriving under low precipitation and high temperature variability. Other tree species include pistachio (Pistacia atlantica), wild almond (Amygdalus scoparia), wild pear (Pyrus glabra), and maple (Acer monspessulanum). The combination of these species creates woodlands of varying density, from closed-canopy forests in wetter highlands to open savanna-like stands in drier zones. This ecological gradient reflects the adaptability of the Zagros vegetation to diverse environmental conditions (Fairclough, 2019).

Biodiversity in the Zagros Forests extends beyond trees to include a wide range of shrubs, grasses, and herbaceous plants. Many of these species are drought-resistant and play important roles in stabilizing soils and supporting grazing systems. The understory vegetation provides critical fodder for livestock, linking ecological functions directly to pastoral livelihoods. Wildlife is also an integral part of the ecosystem: the forests are home to wild goats (Capra aegagrus), Persian fallow deer (Dama mesopotamica), wolves (Canis lupus), and wildcats (Felis silvestris). Bird species such as partridges, vultures, and eagles are common, while reptiles and amphibians inhabit rivers and wetlands within the forest landscape. This combination of flora and fauna makes the Zagros a biodiversity reservoir, even though it is less species-rich than the Hyrcanian region (Flood et al., 2025).

The ecological services provided by the Zagros Forests are crucial for both local and national sustainability. As the watershed of major rivers, the forests regulate hydrological cycles, ensuring water availability for millions of people downstream. They also reduce soil erosion, which is particularly important in Iran's mountainous terrain where heavy rains can trigger landslides. The oak woodlands act as carbon sinks, sequestering greenhouse gases and mitigating climate change impacts. Furthermore, the forests support pollinators and provide non-timber forest products, including medicinal plants, honey, and nuts, which contribute to local economies. In this way, the Zagros Forests function as ecosystem service providers essential for food security, water supply, and climate resilience (Mehri et al., 2024).

However, the ecological balance of the Zagros is increasingly fragile. Unsustainable grazing, illegal logging, and fuelwood collection reduce forest regeneration, leading to a gradual decline in density and cover. Climate change adds another layer of stress, with prolonged droughts weakening oak populations and making them more vulnerable to pests such as the oak gall wasp (Cynips quercusfolii). The decline of these forests not only threatens biodiversity but also undermines the ecosystem services upon which millions of people depend. Recognizing and protecting the ecological characteristics of the Zagros is therefore not only a conservation priority but also a socio-economic necessity (Karimi et al., 2023).

2.3.3 Pastoralism and Traditional Livelihoods

For centuries, the Zagros Forests have been inseparably linked to the pastoralist cultures of western Iran. Tribes such as the Bakhtiari, Qashqai, Lur, and Kurdish groups have shaped and been shaped by the forest landscapes through systems of nomadic and semi-nomadic pastoralism. These groups practice transhumance, or seasonal migration, moving livestock between winter pastures in the lowlands and summer meadows in the highlands. This cyclical pattern allows for sustainable use of resources, as grazing pressure shifts across altitudes and seasons. The Zagros forests provide critical fodder, water, and shelter during these migrations, functioning not only as ecological support systems but also as cultural backdrops for rituals, songs, and oral traditions that celebrate mobility and resilience (Ghaderi & Henderson, 2012).

Traditional pastoralism has also generated a body of indigenous ecological knowledge that is essential for understanding the sustainable use of the Zagros landscapes. Over generations, pastoralists developed systems for managing grazing intensity, protecting springs, and conserving sacred groves. Certain areas of the forest were left untouched as reserves, while others were used rotationally to prevent overuse. Rituals and customary laws reinforced these practices, embedding ecological stewardship within cultural norms. For example, some tribes considered large oak trees sacred, prohibiting their cutting or damaging. This blend of livelihood necessity and cultural symbolism created a co-evolutionary relationship between people and forests, maintaining ecological balance while ensuring community survival (Khater et al., 2024).

Pastoralism also contributed to the cultural identity of Iran. The seasonal migrations of the Bakhtiari and Qashqai tribes are not only ecological adaptations but also cultural spectacles, celebrated in folklore, music, and film. The Bakhtiari migration, for instance, has been immortalized in ethnographic studies and documentaries, symbolizing endurance and harmony with nature. Handicrafts, carpets, and textiles produced by these groups often draw inspiration from forest motifs, further reinforcing the cultural imprint of the Zagros on Iran's heritage. Tourism in the Zagros often capitalizes on this cultural dimension, with visitors attracted to both the landscapes and the tribal traditions that animate them. Thus, pastoralism is both an economic activity and a cultural practice that enriches the heritage value of the Zagros forests (Leal Filho et al., 2023).

However, traditional pastoralism is under strain from modernization and state policies that promote sedentarization, land privatization, and industrial agriculture. These changes have disrupted migratory routes, weakened traditional ecological knowledge systems, and intensified pressure on forest ecosystems. Many younger generations are abandoning nomadic life, leading to a gradual erosion of pastoralist traditions. At the same time, reduced mobility has concentrated grazing in smaller areas, increasing the risk of overuse and deforestation. Balancing modernization with the preservation of traditional livelihoods is therefore essential. Revitalizing pastoralist practices while integrating them with modern conservation and tourism strategies could offer a pathway toward sustainable forest management in the Zagros (Khosravi Mashizi & Sharafatmandrad, 2023).

2.3.4 Cultural and Historical Significance

The Zagros Mountains and their forests occupy a central place in the historical and cultural narrative of Iran. Archaeological findings reveal that the Zagros region was one of the cradles of early human settlement and agricultural development. Excavations in sites such as Ganj Dareh and Tepe Guran in Kermanshah province have uncovered evidence of domesticated goats and early village life dating back more than 10,000 years. These discoveries suggest that the Zagros forests provided not only the ecological conditions for early agriculture but also the cultural foundations of settled life in Iran. Over the centuries, the forests continued to serve as strategic locations for communities, kingdoms, and empires, acting as both protective barriers and resource bases (Mehri et al., 2024).

In Persian folklore and oral traditions, the Zagros forests are celebrated as landscapes of resilience, abundance, and spiritual power. Local myths frequently ascribe protective qualities to ancient oak trees, which are revered as symbols of endurance and strength. Folklore describes forests as dwelling places for spirits, saints, or legendary figures, reinforcing their sacred status within community life. These traditions are not limited to mythology but extend into daily practices, where specific groves are preserved as sacred spaces for rituals and ceremonies. Such beliefs highlight the forests' role as cultural institutions that transmit values of respect, continuity, and belonging across generations (Karimi et al., 2023).

The symbolism of the oak tree is particularly significant in the cultural imagination of the Zagros. Oaks represent not only physical strength but also moral steadfastness and communal resilience. In Kurdish poetry and song, for example, the oak is often used as a metaphor for endurance in the face of hardship, linking ecological elements with cultural identity. In tribal ceremonies, large oak trees often serve as gathering points for decision-making, storytelling, and spiritual practices. By embedding themselves in both material livelihoods and symbolic systems, oaks have become central to the cultural identity of the Zagros, embodying the deep interconnection between people and forests (Madani et al., 2024).

The Zagros region is also dotted with archaeological and historical sites that underscore its importance as a cultural landscape. Ancient settlements, rock carvings, and sacred shrines are scattered throughout the mountains, testifying to millennia of human–forest interaction. Many of these sites are located within or adjacent to forest areas, blending natural and cultural heritage into unified landscapes. For instance, the Bisotun inscription, a UNESCO World Heritage Site, lies within the Zagros region and illustrates how mountains and forests have long served as backdrops for imperial power and cultural expression. In this way, the Zagros forests are not only ecological assets but also cultural archives, preserving evidence of human creativity, resilience, and adaptation over thousands of years (Liburd & Becken, 2020).

2.3.5 Tourism in the Zagros Forests

Tourism in the Zagros region has gained increasing attention in recent years due to the forests' striking landscapes, rich biodiversity, and cultural traditions. The oak-covered mountains provide a dramatic backdrop for hiking, camping, and nature exploration, offering experiences that contrast sharply with the arid deserts and coastal plains found in other parts of Iran. Attractions such as waterfalls, springs, and alpine meadows draw domestic visitors seeking recreation and relief from urban environments. Provinces like Lorestan,

Kermanshah, and Chaharmahal and Bakhtiari are particularly popular for eco-recreational activities, while parts of Khuzestan and Ilam offer unique forest-river landscapes that appeal to both casual tourists and adventure seekers. These diverse natural assets position the Zagros as one of Iran's most versatile tourism regions (Mehri et al., 2024).

Beyond natural beauty, the Zagros forests are renowned for their cultural tourism potential, particularly in relation to pastoralist and tribal heritage. Visitors are drawn to the traditions of the Bakhtiari, Qashqai, and Kurdish communities, whose seasonal migrations and distinctive cultural practices offer living experiences of Iran's intangible heritage. Tribal festivals, music, handicrafts, and cuisine provide opportunities for immersive cultural encounters that complement the forests' ecological attractions. Cultural tourism in the Zagros thus extends beyond sightseeing, offering a holistic experience where landscapes and lifestyles are intertwined. Properly managed, this form of tourism can generate income for local communities while reinforcing pride in cultural traditions and ecological stewardship (Khosravi Mashizi & Sharafatmandrad, 2023).

Ecotourism also holds considerable promise in the Zagros. The forests' biodiversity, including birdwatching opportunities and endemic plant species, could attract niche markets of international eco-travelers. Activities such as guided trekking, wildlife photography, and educational tours can be designed to minimize ecological impact while maximizing conservation awareness. However, developing ecotourism requires significant investment in infrastructure, training, and marketing. Eco-lodges, interpretive centers, and local guides could transform the Zagros into a model of sustainable tourism, aligning with global best practices and enhancing Iran's international reputation as a responsible tourism destination (Ghaderi et al., 2025).

Despite these opportunities, tourism in the Zagros remains largely unregulated and vulnerable to unsustainable practices. Mass domestic visitation, particularly during holidays, results in overgrazing, waste accumulation, and habitat degradation. The construction of villas and resorts in forested areas has led to deforestation and landscape fragmentation. Additionally, the commercialization of tribal culture risks reducing living traditions to staged performances for tourists, undermining authenticity. Without proper planning, tourism could exacerbate the ecological and cultural vulnerabilities of the Zagros rather than mitigating them. To address these challenges, tourism development must be guided by comprehensive management strategies that integrate conservation, community participation, and sustainability principles (Collins et al., 2019).

2.3.6 Environmental Challenges and Threats

The Zagros Forests face some of the most severe deforestation and degradation pressures in Iran. Estimates suggest that forest cover in the region has declined by more than 50 percent over the last century, primarily due to unsustainable land use. Agricultural expansion, particularly the conversion of oak woodlands into orchards and croplands, remains one of the leading causes of deforestation. Illegal logging for timber and fuelwood further reduces forest density, while unregulated construction such as villas and tourism facilities—fragments habitats and accelerates soil erosion. The cumulative effect is a gradual thinning of oak populations, weakening the ecological integrity of the forests and making them more vulnerable to secondary threats (Baloch et al., 2023).

Overgrazing represents another critical challenge. Millions of livestock, particularly sheep and goats, rely on the Zagros forests for fodder. Traditional systems of transhumance once ensured that grazing pressure was distributed across landscapes and seasons, but modernization and sedentarization have concentrated livestock in fewer areas, intensifying ecological stress. Continuous grazing prevents natural regeneration of oak seedlings, leading to declining forest density and a shift toward shrub-dominated landscapes. This not only undermines biodiversity but also weakens ecosystem services, such as soil stabilization and water regulation, that are vital for downstream agriculture and human settlements (Ghorbani et al., 2023).

Climate change and drought add further stress to the Zagros ecosystems. Rising temperatures and declining precipitation have increased the frequency of forest fires, while prolonged droughts have weakened tree populations, making them more susceptible to pests and diseases. The oak gall wasp (Cynips quercusfolii), for example, has devastated thousands of hectares of Persian oak, contributing to large-scale dieback across several provinces. Climate change also exacerbates desertification in surrounding lowlands, creating feedback loops that intensify ecological fragility. These changes threaten not only biodiversity but also the livelihoods of millions of people who depend on the forests for water, grazing, and agricultural productivity (Madani et al., 2024).

Finally, the Zagros Forests suffer from institutional and governance weaknesses that limit effective conservation. Overlapping responsibilities between agencies, insufficient funding, and weak enforcement of environmental regulations allow destructive practices to persist. Local communities, despite their historical role as custodians of the forests, are often excluded from formal decision-making processes. This governance gap has created a situation where short-term economic activities take precedence over long-term sustainability. Unless these structural challenges are addressed, the Zagros Forests risk entering a cycle of ecological decline that may become irreversible within the coming decades.

2.3.7 Governance and Conservation Efforts

Governance of the Zagros Forests is primarily overseen by national institutions such as the Forests, Range and Watershed Management Organization (FRWO) and the Iranian Department of Environment (DoE). These bodies are tasked with developing policies, enforcing regulations, and implementing conservation programs. In principle, they are responsible for preventing illegal logging, monitoring forest health, and coordinating reforestation initiatives. However, the vast scale of the Zagros, combined with limited financial and human resources, makes enforcement difficult. Many conservation programs remain underfunded, reactive, and fragmented, leaving large portions of the forest vulnerable to degradation despite their recognized ecological and cultural importance (Khosravi Mashizi & Sharafatmandrad, 2023).

In recent years, Iran has introduced national policies aimed at halting deforestation and promoting reforestation. Campaigns such as the "National Plan for Oak Regeneration" have sought to restore degraded areas, while bans on logging in natural forests were implemented in 2017 to curb overexploitation. However, these initiatives often suffer from weak implementation and lack of local engagement. Reforestation projects, for example, sometimes rely on non-native or poorly adapted species, undermining ecological resilience. Similarly, enforcement of the logging ban is inconsistent, with illegal extraction continuing in many provinces. These shortcomings highlight the gap between policy formulation and practical outcomes (Sadeghi & Hazbavi, 2022).

Non-governmental organizations (NGOs) and civil society groups have played an increasingly important role in raising awareness and promoting conservation in the Zagros region. Organizations such as the Persian Wildlife Heritage Foundation and smaller local NGOs engage in educational campaigns, tree-planting initiatives, and advocacy for stronger environmental protections. Community-based groups have also begun experimenting with participatory management models, where local people are involved in decision-making and benefit-sharing. While these efforts are promising, they often operate on limited budgets and face institutional barriers, particularly in terms of formal recognition and integration into national policies (Sadeghi & Hazbavi, 2022).

Local communities themselves remain central to any long-term conservation strategy. For generations, pastoralist groups acted as informal custodians of the forests, embedding ecological stewardship into cultural traditions. However, modern governance structures have largely excluded them from forest management, leading to weakened incentives for conservation. Reintegrating community-based practices into formal governance frameworks could strengthen both ecological outcomes and cultural resilience. Successful models from countries such as Nepal and Mexico suggest that when communities are empowered with rights and responsibilities, conservation outcomes improve significantly. For Iran, combining state policies, NGO initiatives, and community participation offers the most realistic pathway toward effective governance of the Zagros Forests (Mehri et al., 2024).

2.3.8 Toward Sustainable Futures

The long-term sustainability of the Zagros Forests requires a holistic approach that integrates ecological conservation with cultural continuity and socio-economic development. Unlike conventional conservation strategies that focus narrowly on ecological protection, a sustainable future for the Zagros must recognize the forests as living cultural landscapes shaped by millennia of human–environment interactions. This perspective acknowledges that pastoralist traditions, tribal knowledge, and local livelihoods are not threats to be eliminated but resources that can be mobilized for sustainable management. By bridging ecological science with cultural heritage, Iran can create a framework that reflects both global conservation standards and local realities (Niknam et al., 2024).

One critical component of such a framework is the revitalization of pastoral traditions. Seasonal migration and customary grazing practices historically maintained ecological balance by distributing pressure across landscapes and allowing for regeneration. Supporting these practices through legal recognition of pastoral rights, protection of migratory corridors, and integration into forest management plans can help restore sustainability. At the same time, modernization pressures cannot be ignored; policies must adapt traditional systems to contemporary conditions by combining indigenous knowledge with modern ecological monitoring. Such hybrid approaches would not only conserve forests but also strengthen cultural resilience among tribal communities (Haq et al., 2023).

Community-based tourism represents another opportunity for building sustainable futures in the Zagros. Instead of mass, unregulated visitation, tourism could be reoriented toward low-impact, community-led models that highlight both natural beauty and cultural traditions. Tribal homestays, guided treks, and cultural festivals could generate income while reinforcing stewardship values. Revenue-sharing mechanisms would ensure that local people benefit directly from tourism, creating stronger incentives for conservation. International models of ecotourism suggest that when communities are empowered as tourism managers rather than passive recipients, both ecological and social outcomes improve. For the Zagros, this approach could transform tourism into a vehicle for conservation and cultural pride (Gaodirelwe et al., 2020).

At the policy level, sustainable futures require integration with international frameworks such as UNESCO, IUCN, and the Global Sustainable Tourism Council (GSTC). Aligning with these standards would enhance Iran's credibility in global conservation arenas while also attracting technical expertise and funding. More innovatively, incorporating the philosophy of the Rights of Nature could provide a normative foundation for rethinking governance in the Zagros. Recognizing forests as rights-bearing entities would compel policymakers to prioritize ecological integrity alongside human development goals. This aligns with Islamic environmental ethics of stewardship (khalifa) and trusteeship (amanat), offering both cultural legitimacy and global relevance (Cheer et al., 2019; Gaodirelwe et al., 2020).

Finally, education and public awareness must be central to any sustainable future. Schools, universities, and media can play key roles in reframing forests from resources to heritage, instilling values of stewardship in younger generations. National campaigns highlighting the cultural symbolism of oaks, the ecological services of forests, and the threats they face could mobilize broader societal support. Sustainable futures for the Zagros will not emerge from technical interventions alone but from a cultural shift that reimagines forests as shared legacies requiring protection. By combining ecological science, cultural traditions, participatory governance, and ethical innovation, Iran can transform the Zagros into a global model of sustainable forest heritage (Sadeghi & Hazbavi, 2022).

2.4   Lesser-Known Forest Ecosystems in Iran

2.4.1 Introduction to Iran's Secondary Forest Systems

While the Hyrcanian and Zagros forests dominate the ecological and cultural narrative of Iran, the country is also home to several lesser-known forest ecosystems that play crucial roles in biodiversity conservation, climate regulation, and cultural heritage. These include the Arasbaran forests in the northwest, the mangrove (Hara) forests of the Persian Gulf, and the semi-arid woodlands of central and eastern Iran, dominated by pistachio and almond species. Although smaller in extent, these forests provide unique ecological services and sustain distinct cultural and economic practices. They represent the diversity of Iran's forest heritage and demonstrate how ecosystems adapt to vastly different climatic and geographical conditions (Goushehgir et al., 2022).

The ecological value of these secondary forests lies in their ability to preserve habitats and species not found in larger forest systems. For instance, the Arasbaran forests harbor a mix of temperate and semi-arid species, creating a biodiversity hotspot that bridges ecological zones. The Hara mangroves, adapted to saline coastal waters, are critical breeding grounds for fish and migratory birds, while also protecting coastlines from erosion. Semi-arid woodlands, though sparse, support resilient plant communities and provide resources such as pistachios, almonds, and medicinal plants, which are deeply integrated into Iranian agriculture and culture. Each of these forest systems contributes to the overall ecological mosaic of Iran, making them essential complements to the Hyrcanian and Zagros (Ghaderi et al., 2025).

Culturally, these forests hold significant but often overlooked value. The Arasbaran region is rich in folklore and traditional practices, reflecting centuries of coexistence between communities and their environment. The mangroves of the Persian Gulf are tied to fishing traditions and local livelihoods, while central Iran's pistachio groves have shaped agricultural economies and social identities for generations. These forests are not only sources of livelihood but also symbols of adaptation, resilience, and cultural continuity in environments that are often harsh and unforgiving. Recognizing their cultural heritage value elevates them beyond ecological statistics, situating them within broader discussions of identity and heritage in Iran (Baloch et al., 2023).

Despite their importance, secondary forests in Iran receive far less attention in policy and public discourse compared to the Hyrcanian and Zagros systems. Their smaller size and geographic isolation often mean they are left out of national conservation strategies, making them highly vulnerable to overexploitation, pollution, and climate change. Yet, their loss would represent not only an ecological tragedy but also the erosion of unique cultural landscapes. This section therefore explores Iran's secondary forest systems in detail, examining their ecological characteristics, cultural significance, tourism potential, and conservation challenges. By including them in a comprehensive analysis of Iran's forest heritage, the book underscores the necessity of integrated conservation strategies that value all ecosystems, regardless of size or visibility (Abouei & Tavasoli, 2024).

2.4.2 The Arasbaran Forests (Northwest Iran)

The Arasbaran Forests, located in East Azerbaijan Province near the borders of Armenia and Azerbaijan, form one of Iran's most biologically and culturally significant ecosystems. Covering roughly 80,000 hectares, this region has been recognized as a UNESCO Biosphere Reserve since 1976 due to its exceptional biodiversity and ecological role. Geographically, Arasbaran lies at the intersection of the Caucasus and Iranian Plateau, creating a transitional zone where temperate, semi-arid, and montane ecosystems converge. This unique location fosters high ecological diversity and makes Arasbaran a critical node in regional conservation. Its proximity to the Aras River also provides hydrological benefits, linking the forests to broader watershed systems that sustain agriculture and human settlements in northwestern Iran (Suleymanov, 2024).

Ecologically, Arasbaran supports over 1,000 plant species, many of which are rare or endemic to the Caucasus Iran transition zone. Prominent vegetation includes oak, hornbeam, maple, and juniper, interspersed with shrubs such as hawthorn and barberry. The region is particularly renowned for its fruit-bearing plants, including wild pomegranate, apple, and pear, which have been traditionally harvested by local communities. The fauna of Arasbaran is equally rich, featuring over 200 bird species, including pheasants, partridges, and raptors. Large mammals such as brown bears, wolves, and wild goats also inhabit the forests, while the Persian leopard (*Panthera pardus saxicolor*) an endangered species remains a flagship predator of the region. This biodiversity underscores Arasbaran's role as a conservation hotspot within Iran and the greater Caucasus (Fayvush et al., 2023).

Culturally, the Arasbaran forests are intertwined with the lives of Azerbaijani-speaking communities who inhabit the region. These communities maintain traditional livelihoods based on pastoralism, horticulture, and handicrafts, often relying on the forest for fodder, fruits, medicinal plants, and firewood. Folklore, music, and oral traditions reflect deep connections to the forested landscape, while local crafts such as carpet weaving and wood carving often incorporate forest motifs. Seasonal migration practices (*yaylag* and *qishlaq*) remain part of community life, linking Arasbaran to broader patterns of pastoralism seen in the Zagros. The cultural significance of the forests is thus inseparable from their ecological value, forming a living heritage landscape where human identity and environment are deeply interwoven (Løland & Akman, 2025).

Despite its ecological and cultural importance, Arasbaran faces significant conservation challenges. Deforestation caused by overgrazing, illegal logging, and land conversion has reduced forest density, while unregulated tourism adds pressures through waste accumulation and habitat disturbance. Climate change further threatens the region, with rising temperatures and shifting precipitation patterns altering vegetation dynamics. Conservation efforts, led by Iran's Department of Environment and supported by UNESCO, have focused on habitat protection and biodiversity monitoring, but enforcement remains weak due to limited resources. Strengthening community participation and promoting eco-cultural tourism could provide sustainable alternatives, allowing Arasbaran to thrive as both a biodiversity hotspot and a cultural heritage landscape (Karataş et al., 2025).

2.4.3 Mangrove Forests of the Persian Gulf (Hara Forests)

The mangrove forests of the Persian Gulf, locally known as the *Hara* forests, represent one of the most unique and fragile ecosystems in Iran. Found primarily along the coasts of Hormozgan Province, particularly around Qeshm Island, Bandar Khamir, and Sirik, these forests cover an estimated 20,000 hectares. Unlike terrestrial forests, the Hara ecosystem is dominated by the grey mangrove (*Avicennia marina*), a salt-tolerant species adapted to tidal fluctuations and saline waters. These trees thrive in intertidal zones, where their aerial roots (pneumatophores) allow for gas exchange in oxygen-poor soils. The ecological adaptations of mangroves make them vital buffers between land and sea, capable of stabilizing coastlines and protecting against erosion and storm surges (Løland & Akman, 2025).

Ecologically, the Hara forests provide critical habitats for a wide range of species. They serve as nurseries for fish and shrimp, supporting local fisheries that sustain coastal communities. Birdlife is especially abundant: the forests are internationally recognized as a stopover for migratory species, including flamingos, herons, ibises, and the endangered western reef heron (*Egretta gularis*). Reptiles such as turtles and numerous invertebrates also depend on the mangrove ecosystem. The ecological services provided by the Hara forests carbon sequestration, nutrient cycling, and water filtration are disproportionate to their relatively small area, making them one of Iran's most valuable ecosystems in terms of environmental impact per hectare (Lachs & Oñate-Casado, 2020).

The cultural and economic importance of the mangroves is equally significant. For centuries, local communities in Hormozgan have relied on the Hara forests for fishing, honey production, and limited wood harvesting. The mangroves also play a role in cultural traditions, with local folklore attributing mystical qualities to these forests that thrive in saline waters where other plants cannot survive. In recent years, the Hara forests have gained recognition as a tourism destination, particularly on Qeshm Island, which has been designated as a UNESCO Global Geopark. Boat tours through the mangrove channels allow visitors to observe wildlife and experience the unique beauty of the tidal ecosystem, blending ecological appreciation with cultural storytelling (Ghaderi & Henderson, 2012).

Despite their importance, the Hara forests face severe conservation challenges. Coastal development, pollution from oil and shipping industries, and unregulated tourism threaten the delicate balance of the ecosystem. Climate change and rising sea levels pose additional risks, altering salinity levels and threatening mangrove survival. Conservation initiatives led by Iran's Department of Environment and international partners have focused on habitat protection and ecotourism promotion, but enforcement remains weak in the face of economic pressures. Integrating community-based management and sustainable tourism practices offers a promising path forward, allowing the Hara forests to be preserved as both an ecological treasure and a cultural landmark of the Persian Gulf (Baloch et al., 2023).

2.4.4 Semi-Arid Woodlands and Shrub lands

In addition to the Hyrcanian, Zagros, and coastal mangrove systems, Iran is home to extensive semi-arid woodlands and shrublands, particularly in the central and eastern provinces. These ecosystems are dominated by drought-resistant species such as wild pistachio (*Pistacia atlantica*), wild almond (*Amygdalus scoparia*), and juniper (*Juniperus excelsa*), alongside hardy shrubs like Artemisia and Astragalus. Unlike dense forest systems, semi-arid woodlands are characterized by open, scattered tree cover, often resembling savanna landscapes. Their ecological importance lies in their resilience to harsh climates, their role in soil stabilization, and their capacity to support diverse plant and animal communities in regions otherwise prone to desertification (Abdelhak, 2022).

These ecosystems also play a crucial role in biodiversity conservation. Semi-arid woodlands host unique assemblages of flora and fauna adapted to extreme conditions, including rare medicinal plants and drought-tolerant grasses essential for grazing. Wildlife species such as gazelles, wild sheep, foxes, and raptors thrive in these landscapes, while reptiles and small mammals form integral parts of the ecological web. Many of these species are threatened by habitat fragmentation and overexploitation, yet they contribute significantly to Iran's overall ecological diversity. Importantly, the resilience of pistachio and almond trees to water scarcity makes these ecosystems particularly relevant in the context of climate change, offering lessons for sustainable land management in arid and semi-arid regions (Jain et al., 2024).

Culturally and economically, semi-arid woodlands have long sustained local communities. The wild pistachio, for example, has both ecological and symbolic significance in Iran. It is considered an ancestor of the domesticated pistachio (*Pistacia vera*), a globally valuable crop and an integral part of Iran's agricultural identity. Communities have historically relied on these woodlands for fruits, nuts, fuelwood, and medicinal plants, embedding them deeply into rural economies and traditional knowledge systems. Folklore and oral traditions often reference pistachio and almond groves as symbols of sustenance and resilience, reflecting their importance in shaping cultural identity in arid landscapes (Abouei & Tavasoli, 2024).

Despite their resilience, semi-arid woodlands face severe degradation pressures. Overgrazing, fuelwood collection, and land conversion for agriculture have significantly reduced their extent and density. Unsustainable harvesting of pistachio resin and medicinal plants further threatens regeneration. Climate change exacerbates these challenges, intensifying droughts and accelerating desertification in fragile landscapes. Conservation initiatives remain limited, as these ecosystems often receive less attention than the more prominent Hyrcanian or Zagros forests. Yet, their ecological services carbon storage, erosion prevention, and biodiversity conservation make them essential components of Iran's forest heritage. Integrating them into national conservation strategies and promoting community-based stewardship could ensure their survival as both ecological and cultural assets (Karimi et al., 2023).

2.4.5 Biodiversity Significance of Lesser-Known Forests

The lesser-known forest ecosystems of Iran Arasbaran, the Hara mangroves, and the semi-arid woodlands collectively contribute to the country's extraordinary biodiversity. Each represents a distinct ecological niche shaped by geography, climate, and evolutionary history, creating habitats for species not found in the Hyrcanian or Zagros systems. Together, these ecosystems expand Iran's ecological portfolio, making the country a regional biodiversity hotspot in the Middle East. By connecting mountainous, coastal, and arid environments, they form ecological corridors that sustain migratory species and genetic diversity across landscapes. Their conservation is therefore essential not only for Iran's ecological resilience but also for global biodiversity goals (Ansari et al., 2023).

The Arasbaran forests illustrate the importance of transitional zones in maintaining biodiversity. Located at the interface of the Caucasus and Iranian Plateau, they host over 1,000 plant species and provide habitats for iconic fauna such as the Persian leopard and brown bear. These forests also support diverse bird populations, making them critical for avian conservation in Eurasia. By acting as ecological bridges, Arasbaran woodlands connect temperate and semi-arid ecosystems, preserving species assemblages that are unique to this transitional geography. Their designation as a UNESCO Biosphere Reserve underscores their global significance as centers of species richness and ecological adaptation (Romagny et al., 2024).

The Hara mangroves contribute to biodiversity in a very different way, supporting marine, avian, and terrestrial species in a delicate coastal environment. Serving as nurseries for fish and shrimp, they sustain local fisheries and food security for coastal communities. The mangroves also provide habitat for migratory birds such as flamingos, herons, and ibises, making them vital stopovers along the Central Asian flyway. The ecological productivity of these tidal forests is remarkable: although they occupy a small geographic area, they host disproportionately high biodiversity relative to their size. Their role in linking marine and terrestrial ecosystems makes them indispensable for maintaining ecological balance in southern Iran (Rezaei et al., 2025).

The semi-arid woodlands of central and eastern Iran highlight biodiversity under extreme conditions. Despite their sparse appearance, these ecosystems harbor a wide range of species adapted to aridity, including drought-resistant pistachio, almond, and juniper trees, as well as medicinal plants that have been used for centuries in traditional Iranian medicine. Wildlife such as gazelles, wild sheep, and raptors depend on these landscapes, while reptiles and small mammals thrive in their harsh conditions. These woodlands thus represent evolutionary laboratories where species survival strategies are tested against climatic extremes. Protecting them is critical not only for biodiversity conservation but also for enhancing Iran's resilience to desertification and climate change (Nasirian & Naddafi, 2025).

2.4.6 Cultural and Tourism Potential

The Arasbaran forests are especially rich in cultural and tourism potential due to their blend of ecological diversity and Azerbaijani cultural traditions. The region's landscapes of oak, hornbeam, and fruit-bearing trees provide a scenic backdrop for eco-tourism activities such as hiking, birdwatching, and wildlife photography. At the same time, the cultural practices of local communities such as carpet weaving, folk music, and seasonal migration (yaylag and qishlaq) offer unique opportunities for cultural tourism. Tourists visiting Arasbaran can experience both natural beauty and cultural authenticity, making it a prime location for eco-cultural tourism initiatives. With its designation as a UNESCO Biosphere Reserve, Arasbaran could serve as a model for integrated tourism that supports both conservation and community livelihoods (Amloy et al., 2024).

The Hara mangroves of the Persian Gulf represent another promising site for sustainable tourism development. Boat tours through the tidal channels of Qeshm Island allow visitors to witness the unique ecological adaptations of mangroves and observe abundant birdlife, including flamingos and herons. These experiences blend adventure with education, fostering greater awareness of the importance of coastal ecosystems. In addition, the mangroves' proximity to the Qeshm Global Geopark creates synergies between geological, ecological, and cultural attractions, enhancing the island's profile as a sustainable tourism hub. However, realizing this potential requires careful management: unregulated boat traffic, pollution, and mass tourism could easily undermine the delicate ecological balance of the mangrove ecosystem (Haseeba et al., 2025).

The semi-arid woodlands of central Iran also hold untapped tourism potential, particularly through cultural landscapes shaped by pistachio and almond trees. These woodlands are closely tied to agricultural traditions, with pistachio cultivation serving as both an economic mainstay and a cultural symbol of Iranian identity. Agrotourism initiatives could allow visitors to experience traditional harvesting practices, learn about pistachio processing, and engage with local communities. Such projects would diversify rural economies, providing alternatives to unsustainable forest use. Beyond agriculture, the stark beauty of semi-arid landscapes combined with their wildlife and medicinal plants could attract niche markets such as eco-photographers and wellness tourism (Baloch et al., 2023).

Despite these opportunities, the tourism potential of Iran's lesser-known forests remains largely underdeveloped and under-promoted. Most initiatives are small-scale, localized, and lack integration into broader national tourism strategies. Moreover, inadequate infrastructure, weak governance, and lack of marketing have limited their ability to attract international visitors. To harness their full potential, Iran must develop comprehensive eco-cultural tourism strategies that integrate conservation goals, community benefits, and international standards. Such strategies could not only strengthen local economies but also raise awareness of the ecological and cultural value of these overlooked ecosystems, ensuring their recognition alongside the Hyrcanian and Zagros forests (Goushehgir et al., 2022; Hosseini et al., 2025).

2.4.7 Threats and Management Challenges

Despite their ecological and cultural importance, Iran's lesser-known forests face severe and often overlooked threats. The Arasbaran forests, for example, suffer from overgrazing, illegal logging, and agricultural expansion, which fragment habitats and weaken regeneration. Traditional pastoralist practices, once sustainable, have been disrupted by modernization, leading to concentrated grazing pressure and ecological degradation. Furthermore, land conversion for orchards and urban development continues to reduce forest cover. Inadequate enforcement of conservation regulations means that protective measures remain largely on paper, leaving these forests vulnerable to ongoing exploitation (Basnyat et al., 2023).

The Hara mangrove forests face a different set of pressures tied to their coastal location. Industrial expansion along the Persian Gulf, including shipping, oil extraction, and port construction, contributes to pollution and habitat destruction. Plastic waste, oil spills, and untreated sewage directly threaten the mangroves' delicate ecosystems, reducing their capacity to support fisheries and birdlife. Unregulated tourism, particularly boat tours that disturb nesting birds and damage root systems, further exacerbates these challenges. Climate change compounds these risks: rising sea levels and changing salinity threaten the survival of mangroves, which depend on precise tidal balances. Without urgent intervention, the ecological services of the Hara forests could collapse (Khosravi Mashizi & Sharafatmandrad, 2023).

The semi-arid woodlands face chronic degradation driven by overexploitation of their limited resources. Fuelwood collection, overgrazing, and unsustainable harvesting of pistachio resin and medicinal plants have significantly reduced forest density. Desertification, already a major concern in central and eastern Iran, is accelerated by the loss of these woodlands, creating feedback loops of soil erosion, reduced rainfall, and biodiversity decline. Climate change adds further stress by intensifying droughts and shifting vegetation zones, pushing ecosystems beyond their natural thresholds. Unlike the Hyrcanian and Zagros forests, these woodlands often fall outside the scope of national conservation strategies, leaving them especially vulnerable to neglect (Hosseini et al., 2025).

Underlying all these ecological threats are governance and institutional challenges. Lesser-known forests receive limited attention compared to the more iconic Hyrcanian and Zagros systems, resulting in fewer resources for monitoring, enforcement, and community engagement. Fragmented responsibilities among government agencies hinder integrated management, while local communities are rarely involved in formal decision-making. This governance gap perpetuates unsustainable practices and undermines conservation initiatives. To address these challenges, Iran must expand its conservation vision to include all forest ecosystems, not just the most prominent ones. Strengthening legal protections, empowering local communities, and integrating international frameworks will be crucial steps toward ensuring the survival of these secondary but vital ecosystems (Dushkova & Ivlieva, 2024).

2.4.8 Toward Integrated Conservation of All Forest Types

Conserving Iran's forest heritage requires a holistic and integrated strategy that recognizes the diversity of ecosystems across the country. Too often, conservation policies have focused primarily on the Hyrcanian and Zagros systems, given their global visibility and size, while secondary forests such as Arasbaran, Hara mangroves, and semi-arid woodlands remain marginalized. Yet these ecosystems provide unique ecological services and sustain cultural identities that cannot be replaced by other forest types. An integrated national approach would ensure that all forest ecosystems, regardless of size or prominence, are valued as essential components of Iran's ecological and cultural mosaic (Khosravi Mashizi & Sharafatmandrad, 2023).

One of the first steps toward integrated conservation is the development of a national forest inventory and monitoring system that includes all ecosystems. Comprehensive data on forest cover, biodiversity, and ecosystem services are essential for identifying priorities and tracking changes over time. While Iran has conducted surveys of the Hyrcanian and Zagros, much less systematic research has been carried out in Arasbaran, mangroves, and semi-arid woodlands. Expanding scientific monitoring to these regions would provide the evidence base needed to inform effective policy, prevent degradation, and strengthen Iran's contribution to global biodiversity targets (Rafiei et al., 2025).

Integration must also occur at the policy and governance level. A unified legal framework that recognizes the diversity of forest ecosystems would help reduce fragmentation and strengthen enforcement. This should be complemented by decentralization and the empowerment of local communities, whose knowledge and traditions often align with conservation goals. For example, involving fishing communities in mangrove management, or tribal groups in Arasbaran and semi-arid woodlands, could create participatory governance models that combine scientific and indigenous approaches. International experiences show that conservation outcomes are more successful when local people are empowered as custodians rather than excluded as passive beneficiaries (Petriello et al., 2025).

Tourism offers another important opportunity for integrated conservation. By promoting eco-cultural tourism across all forest types, Iran can generate income that supports both conservation and local livelihoods. For instance, eco-lodges in Arasbaran, guided boat tours in the Hara mangroves, and agro-tourism in pistachio groves could diversify the tourism economy while raising awareness of ecological values. Linking these diverse attractions into a national network of "forest tourism circuits" would highlight Iran's ecological diversity to both domestic and international audiences, ensuring that lesser-known ecosystems receive attention and support alongside the Hyrcanian and Zagros (N. Khan et al., 2020).

Finally, integrated conservation must be anchored in ethical and global frameworks. The philosophy of the Rights of Nature (RoN) provides a normative foundation for treating all forests large and small as rights-bearing entities with intrinsic value. This approach resonates with Iran's cultural and religious traditions of stewardship and trusteeship, while also aligning with international discourses on environmental ethics. By adopting an RoN-inspired perspective, Iran could lead in reframing conservation not merely as a technical or economic task, but as a moral responsibility. Such an integrated strategy would protect ecological diversity, strengthen cultural identity, and position Iran as a regional leader in sustainable forest heritage management (Ghaderi et al., 2025).

2.5 Biodiversity and Ecological Services of Iran's Forests

2.5.1 Flora and Fauna Richness

Iran's forests represent a mosaic of biodiversity shaped by varied climates, altitudes, and ecological histories. The Hyrcanian forests, as living relics of the Tertiary period, contain over 3,200 vascular plant species, including approximately 400 endemics. Flagship tree species include the Oriental beech (*Fagus orientalis*), ironwood (*Parrotia persica*), and chestnut-leaved oak (*Quercus castaneifolia*). These forests also serve as habitats for iconic mammals such as the Persian leopard (*Panthera pardus saxicolor*), brown bear (*Ursus arctos*), and red deer (*Cervus elaphus*). Avian richness is equally significant, with over 300 bird species using the Hyrcanian as nesting or migratory stopovers. The combination of ancient evolutionary history and ecological complexity makes the Hyrcanian system one of the most important biodiversity reservoirs in Eurasia (Dering et al., 2021).

The Zagros forests, while less species-rich in trees, are ecologically vital for their oak-dominated woodlands. The Persian oak (*Quercus brantii*) constitutes the backbone of the ecosystem, alongside wild pistachio (*Pistacia atlantica*), wild almond (*Amygdalus scoparia*), and maple (*Acer monspessulanum*). Faunal diversity includes wild goats (*Capra aegagrus*), wild sheep (*Ovis orientalis*), wolves (*Canis lupus*), and smaller carnivores such as wildcats (*Felis silvestris*). Raptors such as eagles and vultures soar over these landscapes, while reptiles and amphibians inhabit rivers and springs within forested valleys. Despite severe deforestation pressures, the Zagros forests sustain millions of rural and nomadic communities, linking biodiversity directly to cultural and economic survival (Karimi et al., 2023).

The lesser-known forest systems add further richness to Iran's biodiversity. The Arasbaran forests in the northwest are transitional zones that combine Caucasian, temperate, and semi-arid flora, with over 1,000 documented plant species and diverse fauna, including the Persian leopard, lynx, and brown bear. The Hara mangroves of the Persian Gulf, dominated by *Avicennia marina*, provide nursery habitats for fish and crustaceans while supporting migratory birds such as flamingos, herons, and ibises. Meanwhile, semi-arid woodlands of pistachio, almond, and juniper species harbor drought-adapted plants and animals, including gazelles, foxes, and reptiles. These ecosystems, though smaller in scale, play unique roles in sustaining biodiversity across ecological extremes (Hariram et al., 2023).

Endemic and endangered species highlight the conservation urgency of Iran's forests. The Persian leopard, critically endangered Caspian turtle (*Mauremys caspica*), and Persian fallow deer (*Dama mesopotamica*) exemplify species whose survival is tied to forest health. Plant endemism is particularly striking in Hyrcanian and Arasbaran forests, where relict species connect modern ecosystems to ancient lineages. Collectively, Iran's forests contribute disproportionately to regional and global biodiversity, functioning as reservoirs of genetic diversity, evolutionary history, and ecological resilience. Their protection is therefore critical not only for Iran's heritage but also for the preservation of global biodiversity (Nasirian & Naddafi, 2025).

2.5.2 Ecosystem Services and Human Well-being

Iran's forests provide a wide array of provisioning services that directly support human well-being. Timber, though increasingly restricted due to conservation policies, has historically been harvested from the Hyrcanian and Zagros forests for construction and fuel. More importantly, forests provide non-timber products that remain critical for rural economies. Wild pistachio resin, almonds, honey, fruits, and medicinal plants are harvested in semi-arid and Zagros regions, sustaining both subsistence needs and local markets. The Hara mangroves contribute indirectly to food security by supporting fisheries, while Arasbaran forests supply fruits such as pomegranate and pear. These provisioning services highlight how forests remain deeply tied to the livelihoods of millions of Iranians, particularly in rural and tribal areas (Rezaei et al., 2025).

Equally important are the regulating services performed by forests, which ensure environmental stability on both local and national scales. The Hyrcanian and Zagros forests play a crucial role in regulating hydrological cycles, protecting watersheds, and reducing soil erosion. The Zagros, for instance, feeds major rivers such as the Karun and Karkheh, which provide water for agriculture and urban settlements across southwestern Iran. Forests also act as carbon sinks, mitigating the effects of greenhouse gas emissions and contributing to global climate regulation. The Hara mangroves provide unique coastal protection, buffering shorelines against storms and stabilizing sediments. Without these regulating services, Iran would face greater vulnerability to floods, droughts, and desertification, all of which threaten national development and food security (Madani et al., 2024).

Forests also offer cultural ecosystem services, which are less tangible but equally vital. They provide spaces for recreation, spirituality, and cultural continuity. The Hyrcanian and Zagros forests are popular destinations for domestic tourism, especially during holidays when families engage in picnicking and seasonal festivals. Tribal communities in the Zagros and Arasbaran integrate forests into rituals, music, and oral traditions, while sacred groves in various regions embody spiritual connections to nature. The mangroves of Qeshm Island have become symbolic of ecological resilience, celebrated through eco-tours that blend environmental education with cultural storytelling. These cultural services demonstrate that forests are not merely resources but living heritage landscapes that anchor identity and memory (Amloy et al., 2024).

Taken together, these ecosystem services link environmental integrity directly to human well-being. By providing food, regulating water and climate, and sustaining cultural values, forests function as life-support systems for both local communities and the nation. Their degradation, therefore, represents not only an ecological loss but also a social and economic crisis. Protecting Iran's forests requires acknowledging this interconnectedness and embedding ecosystem services into national development and policy planning. In this sense, forests are not optional environmental amenities but foundational elements of Iran's long-term sustainability and resilience (Haq et al., 2023).

2.5.3 Forests and Climate Resilience

Iran's forests play a pivotal role in mitigating climate change by acting as carbon sinks. The dense canopies of the Hyrcanian forests, with their ancient beech, hornbeam, and oak species, store substantial amounts of carbon, reducing greenhouse gas concentrations in the atmosphere. The Zagros oak woodlands, though less dense, cover a vast geographic area and collectively contribute significantly to carbon sequestration. Even the smaller semi-arid woodlands, dominated by pistachio and almond trees, store carbon in their hardy biomass and extensive root systems. These carbon storage functions help offset emissions from agriculture, industry, and energy production in Iran, linking local forest conservation to global climate mitigation goals (Ernst et al., 2025).

Beyond carbon storage, forests enhance adaptation to climate variability by stabilizing ecosystems and human livelihoods. The Hyrcanian forests regulate rainfall patterns and groundwater recharge in the Caspian basin, reducing the severity of floods and droughts. The Zagros forests protect soils from erosion, sustaining fertile valleys and ensuring water flows to major rivers critical for agriculture in southwestern Iran. In coastal regions, mangrove forests act as natural buffers against storm surges and sea-level rise, reducing risks for vulnerable fishing communities. Semi-arid woodlands, while sparse, slow desertification processes and prevent the spread of sand dunes into agricultural lands. These adaptive functions highlight how forests act as "green infrastructure" for climate resilience (Jong, 2024).

The interaction between forests and climate stressors is increasingly evident in Iran. Climate change has already intensified droughts, pest outbreaks, and wildfires, undermining forest health. In the Zagros, oak dieback caused by pests such as the oak gall wasp has been exacerbated by prolonged drought and rising temperatures. Similarly, the Hyrcanian forests face heightened fire risks, while mangroves are threatened by salinity changes linked to climate variability. Yet, the very forests under stress remain among the most effective defenses against climate change impacts. Their loss would not only reduce biodiversity but also weaken Iran's capacity to adapt to environmental extremes, making conservation an urgent national priority (Nasirian & Naddafi, 2025).

To strengthen ecosystem-based climate strategies, Iran must integrate forest conservation into national climate policies. Expanding reforestation programs, restoring degraded oak and pistachio woodlands, and protecting mangroves are essential steps for enhancing resilience. International frameworks such as REDD+ (Reducing Emissions from Deforestation and Forest Degradation) provide opportunities for Iran to access funding and technical expertise by linking forest management to climate commitments. Moreover, embedding the Rights of Nature framework into policy would ensure that forests are valued not only for their utility but also for their intrinsic role in sustaining climate stability. In this way, Iran's forests can be positioned as both victims of climate change and as solutions to it (Zandebasiri et al., 2023).

2.5.4 Global Significance and Conservation Value

Iran's forests hold global conservation value because they represent unique ecological systems found nowhere else in the world. The Hyrcanian forests, inscribed as a UNESCO World Heritage Site, are among the last surviving temperate broadleaf forests of the Tertiary period, making them a living archive of evolutionary history. The Zagros forests, although less diverse, form one of the largest oak-dominated ecosystems in the Middle East, critical for regional biodiversity and watershed protection. Arasbaran, recognized as a UNESCO Biosphere Reserve, serves as a transition zone between the Caucasus and Iranian Plateau, harboring a distinctive blend of species. The Hara mangroves contribute to global coastal conservation efforts, while semi-arid woodlands showcase species adapted to extreme drought, offering insights into resilience under climate change. Collectively, these ecosystems secure Iran's place as a key custodian of globally significant biodiversity (Walia et al., 2025).

The international importance of Iran's forests extends to their role in migratory species corridors. The Hyrcanian and Arasbaran forests are crucial stopovers for migratory birds traveling along the Eurasian flyways, while the Hara mangroves host thousands of migratory waterbirds each year. These forests also maintain genetic connectivity for large carnivores such as the Persian leopard, linking populations across Iran and into the Caucasus. By sustaining these migratory and wide-ranging species, Iran's forests contribute to global ecological networks that transcend national boundaries. Their degradation would therefore have consequences not only for Iran but also for biodiversity conservation across continents (Rollo, 2025).

Iran's forests also connect directly to international conservation frameworks. UNESCO's World Heritage and Biosphere Reserve designations highlight the global recognition of their importance, while the International Union for Conservation of Nature (IUCN) has identified them as priority areas for conservation. Furthermore, Iran's forests contribute to the objectives of the Convention on Biological Diversity (CBD) and the Sustainable Development Goals (SDGs), particularly those related to life on land (SDG 15), climate action (SDG 13), and sustainable communities (SDG 11). By integrating its forest policies with these global frameworks, Iran has the potential to strengthen international cooperation and attract technical and financial support for conservation initiatives (Sohrabi, 2025).

The global significance of Iran's forests underscores the need for stronger conservation measures and international collaboration. As climate change, deforestation, and habitat fragmentation intensify, these ecosystems face risks that cannot be managed by Iran alone. Partnerships with international organizations, research institutions, and NGOs can provide expertise, funding, and monitoring support to safeguard these ecosystems. At the same time, embedding global recognition within local strategies ensures that conservation efforts remain culturally appropriate and socially inclusive. In this way, Iran's forests can be preserved not only as national treasures but also as vital components of the planet's shared natural heritage (Ansari et al., 2023).

2.6   Tourism and Heritage Forests in Iran

Tourism has emerged as a major force shaping the use and perception of Iran's forests. The Hyrcanian and Zagros systems, along with lesser-known ecosystems such as Arasbaran and the Hara mangroves, serve as key destinations for domestic recreation and, increasingly, for international ecotourism. Their appeal lies in the combination of scenic beauty, biodiversity, and cultural associations that make them attractive year-round destinations. From the lush green landscapes of Mazandaran and Gilan in the north to the oak-covered mountains of Lorestan and Kurdistan in the west, forested regions provide a counterbalance to Iran's arid climate and have become essential spaces for leisure, family gatherings, and seasonal migration. This cultural embeddedness ensures that forests are not only ecological resources but also public spaces of social life (Jong, 2024).

The Hyrcanian forests illustrate both the opportunities and challenges of forest-based tourism. Their recognition as a UNESCO World Heritage Site in 2019 has increased their international visibility, positioning them as potential ecotourism hubs. Yet, domestic visitation dominates, with millions of Iranian tourists traveling to the Caspian provinces during holidays. This influx generates income for local economies but also creates ecological pressures through littering, unregulated camping, and the construction of villas within forest zones. Infrastructure gaps such as waste management systems and eco-friendly accommodations exacerbate these challenges, turning forests into sites of degradation rather than conservation. The paradox of heritage tourism is evident: global recognition raises awareness but also amplifies vulnerability (O'Reilly, 2020).

In the Zagros forests, tourism is closely tied to cultural traditions and tribal heritage. Visitors are attracted not only to the natural beauty of oak woodlands but also to the cultural experiences offered by pastoralist communities such as the Bakhtiari and Qashqai. Tribal migrations, handicrafts, and festivals provide rich cultural dimensions to tourism, transforming the Zagros into a landscape of both natural and cultural heritage. However, unregulated tourism risks commodifying traditions, reducing authentic practices to staged performances. In addition, overgrazing and deforestation caused by human pressures are compounded by mass visitation, further weakening the ecological resilience of the region. Without careful planning, the tourism potential of the Zagros may undermine both cultural integrity and ecological sustainability (Nasirian & Naddafi, 2025).

The Arasbaran forests and Hara mangroves represent niche opportunities for ecotourism. In Arasbaran, hiking, birdwatching, and engagement with Azerbaijani cultural traditions can attract specialized markets. Similarly, the mangrove boat tours around Qeshm Island offer unique experiences of tidal ecosystems and migratory bird habitats, blending adventure with education. However, both ecosystems are fragile and cannot withstand mass tourism. For these areas, the development of small-scale, community-based tourism models is essential to ensure that ecological impacts remain minimal while local people benefit economically. International examples from Latin America and Southeast Asia suggest that eco-cultural tourism can serve as a powerful conservation tool when communities are empowered as managers rather than passive participants (Shokri et al., 2021).

For Iran, the future of forest-based tourism lies in transitioning from mass visitation to sustainable, community-centered tourism. This requires integrated strategies that combine environmental regulation, infrastructure investment, and cultural sensitivity. Visitor education campaigns could foster environmental responsibility, while eco-certification programs could encourage private sector compliance with sustainability standards. At the same time, embedding ethical frameworks such as the Rights of Nature would reframe tourism as an activity that must respect ecological thresholds and intrinsic values. By aligning economic benefits with conservation priorities, Iran could transform its forests into models of heritage tourism where biodiversity, cultural traditions, and visitor experiences reinforce rather than undermine one another (Sadeghi & Hazbavi, 2022).

2.7 Threats and Challenges to Iranian Forest Heritage

Despite their ecological and cultural significance, Iran's forests face a complex array of threats that undermine their status as living heritage. Deforestation and habitat fragmentation are among the most pressing challenges. Agricultural expansion, road construction, and urban sprawl continue to encroach on forest lands, particularly in the Hyrcanian and Zagros regions. Illegal logging, despite recent bans, remains widespread, driven by demand for timber and fuelwood. These activities fragment habitats, disrupt wildlife corridors, and reduce biodiversity, eroding the very values that underpin the designation of forests as natural and cultural heritage. The long-term consequences include not only ecological decline but also the weakening of communities whose livelihoods depend on forest resources (Nasirian & Naddafi, 2025).

Tourism-related pressures exacerbate these problems. While tourism offers opportunities for conservation and economic development, unregulated visitation often leads to ecological degradation. In the Hyrcanian forests, mass tourism has generated significant waste management challenges, with plastics and organic waste accumulating during peak holiday seasons. In the Zagros, the commercialization of tribal traditions risks eroding cultural authenticity while contributing to environmental pressures. In both cases, inadequate infrastructure such as eco-friendly accommodations, designated trails, and visitor education programs intensifies the negative impacts of tourism. Without comprehensive planning, tourism risks transforming heritage landscapes into degraded recreational zones (Niknam et al., 2024).

Climate change further compounds these threats by intensifying droughts, wildfires, and pest outbreaks. The Zagros forests have already experienced widespread oak dieback, linked to a combination of water stress and pest infestations. The Hyrcanian forests face increasing fire risks, while mangroves are threatened by rising sea levels and salinity changes. Semi-arid woodlands, already fragile, are pushed closer to desertification as rainfall declines. These changes not only threaten biodiversity but also undermine the ecosystem services upon which millions of people depend, such as water regulation, soil fertility, and climate mitigation. Climate change thus amplifies existing vulnerabilities, placing Iran's forests under unprecedented stress (Baloch et al., 2023).

Governance and institutional weaknesses represent another critical challenge. Multiple agencies share responsibility for forest management, including the Department of Environment and the Forests, Range, and Watershed Management Organization (FRWO). However, overlapping mandates, limited budgets, and weak enforcement mechanisms hinder effective conservation. Corruption and short-term economic interests often override long-term ecological considerations. Moreover, local communities once central to forest stewardship are frequently excluded from decision-making processes. This governance gap undermines trust, reduces compliance with regulations, and perpetuates unsustainable practices. Strengthening governance is therefore as important as ecological restoration for safeguarding forest heritage (Niknam et al., 2024).

Finally, the marginalization of lesser-known forest ecosystems poses a hidden but significant challenge. While the Hyrcanian and Zagros systems receive some degree of recognition and protection, ecosystems such as Arasbaran, the Hara mangroves, and semi-arid woodlands remain peripheral in national policies. Their smaller size and lower visibility make them particularly vulnerable to neglect, yet their loss would represent an irreplaceable erosion of biodiversity and cultural landscapes. Addressing this imbalance requires a comprehensive approach that values all forests equally as components of Iran's ecological and heritage network. Without such an integrated vision, conservation efforts will remain fragmented, leaving large parts of Iran's forest heritage unprotected (Goushehgir et al., 2022).

2.8 Conclusion

Iran's forests, from the ancient Hyrcanian ecosystems to the oak woodlands of the Zagros, and from the transitional Arasbaran forests to the mangroves and semi-arid woodlands, constitute a mosaic of ecological and cultural heritage. Together, they embody millennia of evolutionary history, sustain extraordinary biodiversity, and provide essential ecosystem services such as water regulation, carbon sequestration, and soil stabilization. Beyond their ecological roles, these forests serve as living landscapes that anchor regional identities, sustain rural livelihoods, and shape the cultural imagination of Iran. Their significance is therefore multidimensional: they are simultaneously ecological assets, economic resources, and cultural symbols.

Tourism adds both opportunities and risks to this heritage. As the Hyrcanian and Zagros forests attract millions of domestic visitors and growing international attention, tourism has the potential to generate income, raise awareness, and support conservation. In Arasbaran and the Hara mangroves, eco-cultural tourism models could diversify local economies while showcasing unique ecological values. Yet, unregulated mass visitation threatens to undermine these same ecosystems, accelerating waste accumulation, habitat disturbance, and cultural commodification. The paradox of forest tourism in Iran reflects a broader global challenge: balancing economic benefits with ecological integrity and cultural authenticity.

The challenges facing Iran's forests are formidable. Deforestation, overgrazing, and land conversion continue to reduce forest cover, while climate change intensifies droughts, wildfires, and pest outbreaks. Governance weaknesses fragmented institutions, underfunding, and limited enforcement further undermine conservation. These challenges highlight that forest heritage is not static but in transition, shaped by dynamic interactions between ecological processes, human activity, and global pressures. Without effective intervention, this transition risks becoming one of decline, where heritage landscapes are degraded beyond recovery.

At the same time, these challenges present opportunities for rethinking forest governance and management. Strengthening community participation, adopting international frameworks (UNESCO, IUCN, CBD), and aligning tourism with sustainability standards can transform forests into models of integrated conservation. Concepts such as the Rights of Nature provide ethical foundations for reframing forests as entities with intrinsic rights, shifting governance from a utilitarian to a stewardship-based approach. This normative shift resonates with Iranian cultural and religious traditions of trusteeship, providing a culturally legitimate pathway for innovation in conservation.

In conclusion, Iran's forests stand at a crossroads between degradation and renewal. As living heritage, they embody the deep interconnection between ecology, culture, and human well-being. Their future depends on whether Iran can integrate ecological science, cultural traditions, community-based management, and ethical innovation into a coherent strategy of conservation. By embracing this integrated vision, Iran has the potential not only to safeguard its forests for future generations but also to position itself as a global leader in the protection of heritage forests in the face of twenty-first-century challenges.

CHAPTER 3

Tourism Development and Environmental Challenges in Iran's Heritage Forests

3.1 Introduction

Tourism has become one of the fastest-growing sectors in Iran's forested regions, reshaping landscapes, economies, and cultural practices. The Hyrcanian, Zagros, Arasbaran, and Hara mangrove forests increasingly serve as destinations for recreation, domestic travel, and, to a lesser extent, international ecotourism. These ecosystems attract visitors for their natural beauty, biodiversity, and cultural richness, offering relief from the arid and semi-arid environments that dominate much of the country. The forests' accessibility from urban centers such as Tehran, Tabriz, and Shiraz further reinforces their popularity, making them central to Iran's tourism geography. Yet, as visitor numbers grow, so too do questions about the sustainability of tourism and its compatibility with long-term forest conservation (Ghorbani et al., 2023).

Tourism in forests presents a fundamental paradox: it is simultaneously a driver of conservation and a source of ecological degradation. On the one hand, tourism generates economic incentives for preservation, raises awareness about ecological and cultural heritage, and can provide alternative livelihoods for local communities. On the other hand, unregulated tourism threatens the very ecosystems it depends upon through waste generation, habitat disturbance, and uncontrolled land-use change. This duality is especially pronounced in Iran, where forest ecosystems are fragile, governance is often fragmented, and infrastructure is inadequate to handle mass visitation. The challenge is therefore to reconcile the benefits of tourism with its ecological costs, ensuring that development does not erode the heritage value of forests (S. Zhang et al., 2023).

The rise of tourism in Iranian forests reflects broader global trends in nature-based and heritage tourism. Worldwide, UNESCO World Heritage status has been shown to attract increasing numbers of visitors, often outpacing the capacity of ecosystems to absorb them. Iran is no exception: the inscription of the Hyrcanian forests on the UNESCO World Heritage List in 2019 has boosted their visibility, fueling both domestic and international interest. Similarly, Qeshm Island's Hara mangroves, as part of a UNESCO Global

Geopark, have gained attention from ecotourists. However, as international experience demonstrates, global recognition without sustainable management frameworks can accelerate degradation rather than safeguard heritage. Iran's forests are thus situated within a wider debate about how heritage sites can be protected while remaining accessible (Sengar & Shah, 2025).

At the national level, forest tourism is deeply embedded in domestic cultural practices. For many Iranians, forests are associated with leisure and social life, particularly through the tradition of picnicking and family outings during holidays. This cultural practice ensures a steady flow of visitors, even in regions with limited infrastructure. While such activities strengthen cultural ties to forests, they also create ecological pressures, including littering, soil compaction, and disturbance of wildlife. The intersection of cultural traditions and environmental impacts underscores the need for tailored strategies that respect social practices while minimizing ecological harm (Hariram et al., 2023).

This chapter examines the relationship between tourism and Iran's forests through the lens of environmental challenges. It begins by analyzing tourism trends in different forest regions, before exploring the specific ecological pressures associated with mass visitation, land-use change, and infrastructure development. Cultural impacts on forest communities are also considered, alongside case studies that illustrate the tensions between economic opportunity and ecological sustainability. Finally, the chapter outlines pathways toward sustainable tourism, highlighting the role of governance, community participation, and international frameworks. In doing so, it positions tourism not merely as an external threat but as a dynamic force that, if managed properly, could become a cornerstone of forest conservation in Iran (Nasirian & Naddafi, 2025).

3.2 Tourism Trends in Iran's Forest Regions

Tourism in Iran's forests is shaped primarily by domestic demand, which accounts for most visitors. The Hyrcanian and Zagros forests are especially popular among urban populations seeking recreation, fresh air, and scenic landscapes. During Nowruz (the Persian New Year) and other national holidays, millions of Iranians travel to northern provinces such as Mazandaran, Gilan, and Golestan, where the Hyrcanian forests provide a striking contrast to the dry central plateau. These domestic flows are deeply tied to cultural traditions such as family picnicking, camping, and seasonal travel, making them both predictable and intense. The cultural embeddedness of domestic tourism ensures its resilience but also creates sustained ecological pressures on fragile forest ecosystems (Haseeba et al., 2025).

International tourism, though smaller in scale, is slowly expanding in Iran's forested regions, driven by global recognition of their heritage value. The inscription of the Hyrcanian forests as a UNESCO World Heritage Site in 2019 and Qeshm Island's designation as a UNESCO Global Geopark have attracted niche groups of international ecotourists, researchers, and conservation enthusiasts. Visitors from Europe and East Asia, in particular, are drawn to Iran's unique biodiversity and cultural landscapes. However, international arrivals remain limited by broader political and infrastructural challenges, including visa restrictions, international sanctions, and limited eco-tourism facilities that meet global standards. As such, Iran's forests remain primarily a domestic tourism resource, with international potential largely untapped (Bui et al., 2020).

The Hyrcanian forests stand at the center of Iran's tourism map due to their accessibility and UNESCO status. Proximity to Tehran and other major cities makes them a prime destination for weekend and holiday travel, leading to seasonal surges in visitor numbers. Tourism here is dominated by short-term recreational activities such as picnicking, camping, and villa stays. In contrast, the Zagros forests attract visitors interested in both natural beauty and cultural experiences. The tribal heritage of Bakhtiari, Qashqai, and Kurdish communities provides a strong cultural dimension to Zagros tourism, with festivals, handicrafts, and migrations forming part of the visitor experience. Unlike the Hyrcanian forests, which are driven by mass domestic visitation, Zagros tourism tends to be smaller in scale but culturally richer (Fairclough, 2019).

The Arasbaran forests in the northwest and the Hara mangroves of the Persian Gulf represent emerging destinations with niche appeal. In Arasbaran, the combination of biodiversity and Azerbaijani cultural traditions has created potential for eco-cultural tourism, though infrastructure remains underdeveloped. The Hara mangroves, especially around Qeshm Island, are better integrated into the tourism economy, with boat tours, birdwatching, and educational excursions increasingly popular among both domestic and international tourists. These ecosystems highlight the diversity of Iran's tourism geography, where each forest type attracts visitors for distinct ecological and cultural reasons. However, their limited carrying capacity means that even modest increases in visitation could pose risks if not carefully managed (Bieling et al., 2020).

Overall, tourism trends in Iran's forests reveal a dual pattern: mass domestic tourism concentrated in the Hyrcanian and Zagros, and niche ecotourism emerging in Arasbaran and mangrove ecosystems. This duality reflects both opportunities and vulnerabilities. While domestic tourism ensures steady demand and cultural engagement, it also places immense pressure on ecosystems. International tourism, though limited, holds potential for diversification and conservation-oriented development, but requires substantial investment in infrastructure, governance, and global marketing. Understanding these trends is crucial for designing strategies that harness the benefits of tourism while mitigating its ecological and cultural costs (Leal Filho et al., 2023).

3.3 Environmental Pressures from Tourism

Tourism in Iran's forest ecosystems generates significant waste management challenges, particularly during peak holiday seasons when visitor numbers surge. The cultural tradition of outdoor picnicking, while socially valuable, often leads to the accumulation of plastics, food waste, and disposable utensils within forest landscapes. In the Hyrcanian forests, plastic bottles, bags, and food packaging are commonly left behind, creating long-term environmental hazards as they enter soil and waterways. Organic waste, though biodegradable, disrupts wildlife feeding patterns by attracting scavengers and altering ecological balances. The lack of adequate waste disposal infrastructure such as bins, recycling systems, and waste collection services exacerbates the problem, transforming tourism into a major source of pollution (Amloy et al., 2024).

Beyond waste, tourism contributes to deforestation and habitat fragmentation. The construction of villas, resorts, and access roads in forested areas, particularly in Mazandaran and Gilan provinces, has led to the conversion of forest lands into residential and recreational spaces. Informal land use, often driven by private investment and weak enforcement of regulations, has fragmented habitats, reducing connectivity for wildlife such as leopards, bears, and deer. Off-road driving and unregulated camping also damage vegetation cover, compact soils, and disturb fragile understorey ecosystems. Over time, these practices undermine the ecological resilience of forests, leaving them less capable of regenerating and sustaining biodiversity (Dering et al., 2021).

Wildlife disturbance is another significant pressure resulting from forest tourism. Large mammals such as the Persian leopard, brown bear, and wild goats are increasingly threatened by human presence, noise, and habitat encroachment. Tourist activities including hiking, camping, and boating in mangrove areas often bring humans into proximity with wildlife, leading to behavioral changes such as altered feeding patterns, displacement from habitats, or increased human–wildlife conflict. Bird populations are particularly vulnerable: migratory species resting in the Hara mangroves or Arasbaran forests may abandon nesting sites when exposed to repeated disturbances from boats or large groups of visitors. This disturbance not only affects species survival but also weakens the ecological integrity of forest systems (Khosravi Mashizi & Sharafatmandrad, 2023).

Tourism also places pressure on water and soil resources in forested regions. Increased demand for water to support tourism, infrastructure, hotels, resorts, and recreational facilities competes with local community needs and ecological requirements. In the Hyrcanian and Zagros regions, over-extraction of water has intensified pressure on rivers and aquifers, particularly during dry summers. Soil degradation is equally problematic: trampling by large numbers of visitors leads to compaction, reduced infiltration, and erosion on forest trails and camping sites. The construction of tourism facilities without proper land-use planning further accelerates erosion, landslides, and sedimentation in waterways, diminishing the forests' ability to regulate hydrological cycles (Rezaei et al., 2025).

The cumulative effects of these environmental pressures highlight the unsustainable trajectory of tourism in Iran's forests. Without effective management, forests risk shifting from being assets for tourism to victims of its expansion. The irony is that the very qualities that attract visitors clean air, rich biodiversity, scenic landscapes are being undermined by uncontrolled tourism practices. Addressing these pressures requires both infrastructural investment (waste management, eco-friendly facilities) and regulatory reforms (land-use enforcement, visitor limits). It also demands cultural shifts, where visitors are educated to see forests not simply as recreational backdrops but as fragile ecosystems requiring respect and stewardship (Mehri et al., 2024).

3.4 Tourism Infrastructure and Land-Use Change

Tourism expansion in Iran's forest regions has been closely tied to the growth of infrastructure, including roads, villas, hotels, and recreational facilities. While infrastructure development is often framed as a prerequisite for economic growth, in forest ecosystems it frequently comes at the expense of ecological integrity. In the Hyrcanian region, road construction to connect urban centers with forested holiday destinations has fragmented habitats, increasing vehicle access and opening once remote areas to mass visitation. These roads not only disrupt wildlife corridors but also facilitate illegal logging and land conversion. Infrastructure designed to support tourism often accelerates ecological degradation rather than creating controlled and sustainable access (Scheyvens & van der Watt, 2021).

The most visible form of land-use change in forest tourism is the construction of private villas and resorts, particularly in the northern provinces of Mazandaran and Gilan. These villas, often built without proper environmental assessments, encroach directly on forest lands, displacing vegetation and wildlife habitats. Their proliferation reflects both domestic demand for leisure properties and weak enforcement of land-use regulations. As forests are converted into residential areas, their capacity to provide ecosystem services such as water regulation, carbon sequestration, and soil stabilization is diminished. This trend illustrates the structural imbalance between short-term economic gains from tourism real estate and the long-term ecological sustainability of heritage forests (Dushkova & Ivlieva, 2024).

In the Zagros forests, infrastructure pressures take different forms. While villa construction is less widespread, the expansion of rural roads, small-scale resorts, and facilities for cultural tourism has disrupted tribal migration routes and grazing patterns. Pastoralist communities, whose livelihoods are already under stress from modernization, face additional challenges when traditional land-use systems are replaced by tourism infrastructure. The result is not only ecological fragmentation but also cultural disruption, as tourism reshapes landscapes that have historically sustained both biodiversity and human traditions. The conversion of tribal lands into tourism zones risks eroding the very cultural authenticity that attracts visitors in the first place (Basnyat et al., 2023).

The Hara mangroves face infrastructure pressures linked to tourism boating and coastal development. The construction of docks, boat-launching sites, and recreational facilities on Qeshm Island and nearby areas has altered tidal flows and damaged mangrove root systems. Similarly, in the Arasbaran forests, unregulated eco-lodge construction and expansion of rural tourism facilities are beginning to affect fragile habitats. These cases highlight how tourism-driven infrastructure, even when relatively small in scale, can have disproportionate impacts on ecosystems that are ecologically sensitive and geographically limited. The problem is compounded by the absence of integrated land-use planning and weak coordination between tourism and environmental authorities (Haseeba et al., 2025).

The underlying issue is governance gaps in land-use regulation and enforcement. Multiple institutions including the Ministry of Tourism, the Department of Environment, and local municipalities have overlapping but poorly coordinated responsibilities. This fragmentation creates loopholes that allow illegal construction, unregulated development, and land conversion to persist. Corruption and short-term profit motives often further weaken enforcement. Without a coherent governance framework that integrates tourism planning with environmental sustainability, infrastructure expansion will continue to degrade Iran's forest heritage. Effective solutions require not only stricter legal enforcement but also community-based land-use planning that balances tourism opportunities with ecological thresholds (Croker et al., 2023).

3.5 Cultural Impacts of Tourism on Forest Communities

Tourism in Iran's forest regions not only transforms landscapes but also reshapes the cultural fabric of local and tribal communities. In the Zagros and Arasbaran regions, tourism is closely tied to pastoralist and tribal traditions. Visitors are drawn to seasonal migrations, music, handicrafts, and cuisine, which are presented as authentic cultural experiences. However, the commercialization of these traditions often reduces them to staged performances designed for tourists rather than living practices rooted in community life. This process of commodification risks eroding the integrity of cultural expressions, turning them into spectacles that prioritize tourist demand over cultural continuity. The very practices that once sustained cultural resilience risk being hollowed out by market forces (Liburd & Becken, 2020).

Changes in livelihood patterns are another cultural impact of tourism. For many forest communities, tourism offers alternative sources of income, from guiding and handicraft sales to homestays and eco-lodges. While this diversification can reduce reliance on extractive practices such as logging or overgrazing, it also shifts community economies toward service-oriented activities. Younger generations are more likely to abandon pastoralist traditions in favor of tourism-related work, leading to a gradual decline in the transmission of indigenous ecological knowledge. The short-term economic benefits of tourism therefore come with long-term cultural trade-offs, as communities adapt to the demands of a tourism economy (Cárcamo Macoto et al., 2024).

Tourism can also create social tensions within communities. The benefits of tourism are rarely distributed equally, with wealthier households or those located near popular tourist sites more likely to profit. This uneven distribution can exacerbate existing inequalities and fuel conflicts over land use and resource access. In some cases, tourism has accelerated land privatization, restricting access to pastures and forests traditionally managed as common. For pastoralist groups, this loss of collective resource governance undermines not only livelihoods but also cultural values of cooperation and reciprocity. Tourism thus reshapes social dynamics, creating both opportunities and divisions within forest-dependent communities (Bui et al., 2020).

At the same time, tourism provides opportunities for cultural revitalization and pride when managed inclusively. Community-based tourism initiatives in the Zagros and Arasbaran regions have demonstrated that when local people are empowered as managers, tourism can reinforce rather than erode traditions.

For example, showcasing handicrafts, cuisine, and storytelling within community-led frameworks allows cultural practices to be celebrated on local terms. Similarly, tribal music and festivals, when presented in authentic contexts, can foster intergenerational transmission of knowledge and strengthen cultural identity. These cases highlight that the cultural impacts of tourism are not predetermined but depend on governance models and community participation (Jagielska-Burduk et al., 2021).

Ultimately, the cultural impacts of tourism in Iran's forests reflect the tension between preservation and transformation. On one hand, tourism has the potential to revitalize traditions, provide income, and increase recognition of cultural heritage. On the other hand, it risks commodifying, fragmenting, and transforming community practices in ways that undermine their authenticity. The challenge lies in striking a balance where tourism supports cultural continuity without reducing heritage to a market commodity. This requires an approach that ensure communities have agency in how their traditions are represented and integrated into tourism. Only through such models can tourism contribute to both cultural vitality and ecological stewardship in Iran's forest regions (Iskakova et al., 2021).

3.6 Case Studies of Environmental Degradation Linked to Tourism

3.6.1 Hyrcanian Forests: Holiday Waste and Villa Construction

The Hyrcanian forests of northern Iran are the country's most popular forest tourism destination, attracting millions of visitors annually, particularly during Nowruz and summer holidays. This intense visitation generates enormous volumes of waste, much of it plastic and disposable items, which local municipalities lack the capacity to manage. Forest clearings and riverbanks are often littered after holiday seasons, disrupting ecosystems and creating long-term pollution. Wildlife is affected as scavengers feed on food waste, altering feeding behaviors and increasing human–wildlife encounters. Soil compaction and vegetation loss along popular picnic sites further degrade the ecological quality of the forests (Mehri et al., 2024).

In addition to waste, the Hyrcanian region faces rapid villa construction driven by tourism demand. Forested lands in Mazandaran and Gilan have been illegally converted into private holiday properties, fragmenting habitats and reducing forest cover. Weak enforcement of land-use laws allows this trend to continue, with short-term economic profits prioritized over ecological sustainability. The result is double pressure: mass tourism that degrades forests from within and real estate development that consumes forests from the outside. Together, these processes threaten the ecological integrity of the

Hyrcanian forests despite their UNESCO World Heritage recognition (Rafiei et al., 2025).

3.6.2 Zagros Forests: Tribal Culture and Overgrazing–Tourism Overlap

The Zagros forests, rich in both biodiversity and tribal heritage, attract tourists seeking cultural experiences with Bakhtiari, Qashqai, and Kurdish communities. However, the commercialization of tribal culture for tourism has unintended ecological consequences. Tribal festivals and migration spectacles, when staged for tourists, often involve large gatherings that generate waste, increase demand for firewood, and place additional pressure on local ecosystems. This tourism-driven commodification not only risks diluting cultural authenticity but also amplifies ecological pressures in regions already struggling with deforestation and oak dieback (Khosravi Mashizi & Sharafatmandrad, 2023).

Tourism in the Zagros also intersects with overgrazing, one of the most serious threats to the ecosystem. Visitors often arrive during grazing seasons, compounding the stress on fragile oak regeneration zones. Tourism infrastructure roads, picnic areas, and campsites reduce the space available for grazing, leading to concentrated livestock pressure in smaller areas. This overlap between tourism and pastoralism accelerates degradation, creating conflicts between conservation goals, tourism development, and local livelihoods. The case of the Zagros highlights how tourism pressures can exacerbate pre-existing ecological vulnerabilities when not integrated into broader land management strategies (Shokri et al., 2021).

3.6.3 Hara Mangroves: Ecotourism and Habitat Disturbance

The Hara mangrove forests around Qeshm Island illustrate the fragility of coastal ecosystems under tourism pressure. Boat tours through mangrove channels, a popular activity for both domestic and international visitors, often disturb nesting birds and damage mangrove roots. The noise and physical presence of boats disrupt the feeding and breeding behaviors of bird species such as herons, flamingos, and ibises. Repeated disturbances can cause birds to abandon key habitats, undermining the ecological value of the mangroves as internationally significant stopovers for migratory species (Ghorbani et al., 2023).

Beyond wildlife disturbance, tourism infrastructure in the mangroves contributes to ecological stress. The construction of docks, piers, and recreational facilities alters tidal flows and accelerates erosion, weakening the natural resilience of the mangroves. Waste disposal from tourism activities further contaminates water quality, reducing the forests' capacity to support fisheries and other ecosystem services. The Hara case underscores that even activities labeled as ecotourism can become sources of degradation if not carefully regulated and monitored. Sustainable management, including strict visitor limits and community-led monitoring, is essential to balance ecotourism with conservation (Mehri et al., 2024).

3.7 Toward Sustainable Tourism in Forest Regions

Tourism in Iran's forests must shift from mass visitation to sustainability-oriented models if it is to support rather than undermine conservation. Current patterns characterized by unmanaged waste, villa construction, and habitat disturbance illustrate the risks of unregulated tourism. A transition to sustainable tourism requires integrating ecological thresholds into planning, setting visitor capacity limits, and developing infrastructure that minimizes environmental impact. This transformation is not only a technical necessity but also a cultural and political challenge, as it demands balancing the desires of domestic tourists, the needs of local communities, and the imperatives of conservation (Rezaei et al., 2025).

Ecotourism provides one of the most promising pathways for sustainable development in forest regions. Unlike mass tourism, ecotourism emphasizes small-scale, low-impact activities that promote environmental awareness and support local livelihoods. In the Hyrcanian forests, for example, guided nature walks, birdwatching, and educational tours could replace mass camping and picnicking as dominant practices. In Zagros, eco-cultural tourism centered on authentic tribal experiences managed by communities themselves could generate income while reinforcing cultural identity. The Hara mangroves are ideally suited to boat-based ecotourism, provided strict controls are implemented to prevent wildlife disturbance. These models demonstrate how tourism can align with conservation goals when carefully designed (Nathaniel & Adedoyin, 2022).

International experiences offer valuable best practices for Iran. Countries such as Costa Rica, Nepal, and Bhutan have shown that community-based ecotourism can generate sustainable income while protecting biodiversity. Key lessons include establishing eco-certification systems, training local guides, and reinvesting tourism revenues into conservation projects. For example, Costa Rica's national park system funds local development through visitor fees, while Bhutan's high-value, low-volume tourism model prevents overcrowding. These experiences demonstrate that tourism can become a tool for both conservation and socio-economic resilience, provided strong governance frameworks are in

place. Iran, with its combination of cultural richness and ecological diversity, is
well-positioned to adapt such models (Walia et al., 2025).

Education and awareness are critical for embedding sustainability into
tourism practices. Visitor education campaigns, signage in forests, and media
outreach can shift public perceptions of forests from recreational backdrops to
fragile ecosystems requiring respect. Schools and universities can also play a
role by integrating environmental education into curricula, ensuring future
generations understand the ecological and cultural significance of Iran's forests.
By cultivating environmental stewardship among tourists, sustainable tourism
can become a cultural norm rather than a niche practice (Croker et al., 2023) .

Ultimately, achieving sustainable tourism in Iran's forests requires a multi-
level governance strategy. National policies must integrate tourism with
environmental planning, local communities must be empowered as active
managers, and private sector actors must adopt eco-certification and
sustainability standards. International partnerships can provide technical and
financial support, while ethical frameworks such as the Rights of Nature can
anchor tourism in a philosophy of ecological respect. By aligning tourism with
conservation and cultural integrity, Iran can transform its forests into models
of sustainable heritage tourism where economic benefits, ecological protection,
and cultural continuity reinforce one another rather than compete (Petersmann,
2024).

3.8 Policy and Governance Responses

Iran has established a number of policies and institutions intended to
regulate tourism and protect forest environments. The Forests, Range and
Watershed Management Organization (FRWO) and the Department of
Environment (DoE) are the primary agencies responsible for conservation,
while the Ministry of Cultural Heritage, Tourism and Handicrafts oversees
tourism development. In principle, these institutions are meant to coordinate
their efforts, ensuring that tourism aligns with ecological and cultural
sustainability. However, in practice, policies often remain fragmented, reactive,
and poorly enforced. Tourism continues to expand faster than environmental
safeguards, creating a persistent gap between policy goals and on-the-ground
realities (Liburd & Becken, 2020).

One major limitation is the weak enforcement of environmental regulations.
Despite bans on logging in natural forests and restrictions on land conversion,
illegal villa construction and deforestation remain widespread, particularly in the
Hyrcanian region. Corruption, insufficient funding, and limited personnel
undermine the ability of agencies to monitor and regulate land use effectively.

Similarly, policies intended to promote sustainable tourism often lack clear implementation mechanisms, leading to inconsistencies between national strategies and local practices. Without strong enforcement, policies risk being symbolic rather than transformative (Hariram et al., 2023).

Another challenge lies in the lack of community participation in governance. Forest communities pastoralists in the Zagros, Azerbaijani villagers in Arasbaran, or fishing households near the Hara mangroves are rarely included in formal decision-making processes. This exclusion weakens local stewardship and reduces incentives for conservation. Community-based tourism projects exist but remain limited in scale and are often not integrated into broader policy frameworks. International experience demonstrates that when communities are empowered with rights and responsibilities, conservation outcomes improve. Iran's policies have yet to fully embrace this approach, leaving a critical gap in governance (Ansari et al., 2023).

At the same time, international frameworks provide opportunities for strengthening governance. UNESCO's designation of the Hyrcanian forests and Qeshm Geopark, as well as the Arasbaran Biosphere Reserve status, create obligations for Iran to adhere to global conservation standards. Similarly, commitments under the Convention on Biological Diversity (CBD) and the Sustainable Development Goals (SDGs) require Iran to integrate conservation into development planning. These frameworks offer not only normative guidance but also potential access to international funding and technical expertise. The challenge lies in translating international commitments into concrete national and local actions (Leal Filho et al., 2023).

To address these gaps, Iran needs a comprehensive governance reform strategy for forest-based tourism. This should include: (1) strengthening legal enforcement against illegal land conversion and unregulated development, (2) empowering communities through participatory governance and equitable revenue-sharing, (3) aligning national policies with international frameworks to attract external support, and (4) promoting eco-certification and sustainability standards in the private sector. By combining stronger enforcement, community empowerment, and international cooperation, Iran can transform its fragmented policy environment into an integrated governance system capable of balancing tourism growth with environmental sustainability.

3.9 Conclusion

Tourism in Iran's forests embodies both promise and peril. On the one hand, it generates economic opportunities, strengthens cultural recognition, and has the potential to fund conservation. On the other, it poses profound ecological risks when unregulated, from waste accumulation and habitat fragmentation to overexploitation of water and soil resources. The case studies of the Hyrcanian, Zagros, and Hara mangroves illustrate that the very qualities attracting visitors lush landscapes, biodiversity, and cultural traditions are being undermined by unsustainable tourism practices. Unless managed within ecological thresholds, tourism may accelerate the degradation of forests rather than support their preservation.

The analysis of tourism trends reveals a dual pattern: mass domestic visitation concentrated in the Hyrcanian and Zagros regions, and emerging niche ecotourism in Arasbaran and mangrove ecosystems. This duality reflects the complex interplay between cultural traditions, domestic demand, and international recognition. While domestic tourism ensures a steady flow of visitors, it creates significant environmental pressures. International ecotourism offers opportunities for diversification and conservation awareness but requires major investments in infrastructure, governance, and global positioning. Balancing these dynamics is essential for building a sustainable tourism model that benefits both people and forests .

Environmental pressures from tourism are compounded by infrastructure expansion and governance weaknesses. Road construction, villa development, and unregulated resorts fragment ecosystems and displace communities, while overlapping institutional mandates hinder effective regulation. Policies exist but are inconsistently implemented, allowing illegal practices to persist. Without comprehensive land-use planning and stronger enforcement, tourism will continue to reshape forest landscapes in ways that erode both ecological integrity and cultural authenticity. Governance reform, therefore, is as important as ecological restoration in shaping the future of forest tourism.

Yet, tourism also provides a unique opportunity for conservation when managed responsibly. Community-based tourism models can empower local populations, generate equitable income, and reinforce cultural identity. International best practices demonstrate that small-scale, low-impact tourism can enhance biodiversity protection while supporting livelihoods. Education and awareness campaigns further embed stewardship into visitor behavior, transforming tourism from an extractive practice into a conservation tool. By adopting ecotourism principles and aligning with global frameworks such as UNESCO and the Convention on Biological Diversity, Iran can reframe tourism as a partner in heritage preservation rather than a threat.

In conclusion, tourism in Iran's forests stands at a crossroads. Managed through integrated policies, community participation, and ecological safeguards, it can become a driver of sustainability, ensuring forests remain living heritage for future generations. Left unchecked, however, tourism risks accelerating ecological decline and cultural commodification. The path forward requires recognizing tourism's dual nature, embracing its potential while rigorously addressing its risks. By balancing growth with sustainability, Iran can transform its forest regions into models of heritage tourism where ecology, culture, and economy coexist in harmony.

CHAPTER 4

RIGHTS OF NATURE AND SUSTAINABLE TOURISM: A NORMATIVE FRAMEWORK FOR IRAN

4.1 Introduction: Why a New Framework is Needed

Iran's forests stand at a critical juncture. The Hyrcanian, Zagros, Arasbaran, and Hara mangrove ecosystems are not only ecological treasures but also cultural and economic lifelines. Yet, as shown in previous chapters, these forests face mounting pressures from deforestation, overgrazing, climate change, and unsustainable tourism. Despite a range of policies and institutions ranging from logging bans to protected area designations conservation outcomes remain weak. Forest degradation continues, reflecting a mismatch between the scale of ecological challenges and the capacity of existing governance systems. This situation underscores the urgent need for new frameworks that go beyond traditional resource management and embrace holistic, rights-based approaches (Sadeghi & Hazbavi, 2022).

Conventional forest governance in Iran has been largely utilitarian, treating forests as resources to be regulated, extracted, or restored according to human needs. While this paradigm has achieved limited successes, it fails to capture the intrinsic value of ecosystems or the cultural and spiritual connections communities maintain with forests. Moreover, policies often operate in isolation, with forestry agencies, tourism authorities, and conservation bodies working in fragmented ways. This siloed approach limits effectiveness and undermines the possibility of integrated solutions. A new governance framework must move beyond resource-centered thinking to acknowledge forests as living systems with ecological, cultural, and ethical significance (Nathaniel & Adedoyin, 2022).

The Rights of Nature (RoN) paradigm offers one such framework.
Emerging in the 21st century from both legal innovations and indigenous
worldviews, RoN challenges the dominant anthropocentric model by
recognizing ecosystems as rights-bearing entities. From Ecuador's
constitutional recognition of nature's rights to New Zealand's granting of legal
personhood to the Whanganui River, RoN represents a global shift toward
valuing ecosystems not merely for their utility but for their intrinsic worth.
Applying this framework in Iran could reframe forests from objects of
management to subjects of protection, demanding governance approaches that
safeguard their ecological integrity irrespective of short-term economic
pressures (Liburd & Becken, 2020).

The Iranian context provides fertile ground for adopting such a paradigm.
Islamic environmental ethics emphasize stewardship (*khalifa*), trusteeship
(*amanat*), and balance (*mizan*), principles that resonate strongly with the
philosophy of RoN. At the same time, local communities pastoralists, farmers,
and fishing households already embody aspects of rights-based governance
through traditional practices that respect ecological thresholds. By integrating
RoN into Iran's governance of forest tourism, policymakers can align global
discourses with local traditions, creating a culturally legitimate and
internationally relevant framework. This blending of ethics, culture, and law
could provide a powerful foundation for sustainable heritage management
(Nathaniel & Adedoyin, 2022).

This chapter therefore argues for the development of a normative and
practical framework that integrates Rights of Nature into Iran's forest
governance. It begins by reviewing existing national policies and identifying
their gaps, before situating Iran within global discourses on RoN. It then
explores the compatibility between RoN and Islamic stewardship,
demonstrating how ethical traditions can reinforce innovative governance. The
chapter also considers practical applications of RoN to tourism in forests,
highlighting how community participation can serve as a bridge between
normative principles and daily practice. Finally, it proposes a strategic roadmap
for embedding RoN into Iran's policies, laws, and conservation strategies. By
adopting this new framework, Iran has the opportunity to transform its forests
from vulnerable resources into protected heritage with enduring rights.

4.2 National Policy Frameworks and Their Gaps

Iran's forest governance is formally anchored in the mandates of two main
institutions: the Forests, Range and Watershed Management Organization
(FRWO) and the Department of Environment (DoE). The FRWO, under the
Ministry of Agriculture Jihad, is tasked with managing forest resources,

enforcing logging bans, and implementing reforestation projects. The DoE, by
contrast, oversees protected areas and biodiversity conservation. Together,
these institutions are expected to regulate forest use and ensure environmental
sustainability. In practice, however, overlapping responsibilities, limited
coordination, and inadequate budgets have constrained their effectiveness. The
persistence of deforestation, illegal villa construction, and uncontrolled tourism
indicates that existing frameworks fall short of safeguarding Iran's forest
heritage (Hariram et al., 2023).

A major step in policy reform was the 2017 ban on commercial logging in
natural forests, designed to halt decades of overexploitation, especially in the
Hyrcanian system. While symbolically significant, implementation has been
uneven. Illegal logging persists, often facilitated by weak enforcement
mechanisms and local corruption. Moreover, the ban did not adequately address
other drivers of forest loss, such as agricultural expansion and urban sprawl.
Reforestation initiatives, often promoted as compensatory measures, have also
faced criticism for relying on non-native or poorly adapted species, reducing
ecological effectiveness. These shortcomings reveal a recurring pattern in Iran's
forest policy: ambitious declarations undermined by practical and structural
constraints (Flood et al., 2025).

Tourism policy adds another layer of complexity. The Ministry of Cultural
Heritage, Tourism and Handicrafts promotes tourism development as a driver
of economic growth, but often with little consideration for ecological
thresholds. In the northern provinces, unregulated tourism has led to the
proliferation of villas and resorts within forest zones, undermining conservation
efforts by the FRWO and DoE. The lack of integrated planning means that
tourism and conservation policies frequently work at cross-purposes, with one
institution incentivizing expansion while another attempts to enforce
restrictions. This institutional dissonance highlights a fundamental governance
gap: the absence of a coherent framework linking tourism growth to
environmental sustainability (Croker et al., 2023).

Another limitation of Iran's policy landscape is the exclusion of local
communities from decision-making. Historically, pastoralist groups in the
Zagros or fishing communities near the Hara mangroves managed ecosystems
through customary norms and taboos that ensured long-term sustainability.
Modern governance structures, however, have largely displaced these systems,
concentrating authority in centralized institutions. Community participation in
policy is minimal, often limited to consultation rather than genuine power-
sharing. This exclusion reduces compliance with conservation rules and erodes
local incentives to protect forests, further weakening governance outcomes
(Kurbiyanto et al., 2024).

Finally, Iran's forest policies lack adequate integration with global frameworks and climate strategies. Although Iran is party to the Convention on Biological Diversity (CBD) and has UNESCO-recognized sites such as the Hyrcanian forests, these commitments remain weakly reflected in national strategies. For instance, tourism in World Heritage sites is not systematically monitored, nor are biodiversity indicators regularly updated. Similarly, climate adaptation policies rarely incorporate forests as central pillars of resilience. The gap between international commitments and national implementation undermines Iran's credibility and deprives it of opportunities for international funding and technical cooperation. Bridging these gaps will require structural reforms that align national policies with both local realities and global conservation obligations.

4.3 Global Discourses on Rights of Nature (RoN)

The concept of the Rights of Nature (RoN) emerged as a response to the limitations of conventional environmental law, which traditionally views ecosystems as property to be regulated for human benefit. Instead, RoN asserts that nature itself rivers, forests, mountains, and entire ecosystems possesses intrinsic rights to exist, regenerate, and evolve. This paradigm shift reflects a move from anthropocentric (human-centered) to Eco-friendly (nature-centered) perspectives, challenging the legal and ethical foundations of environmental governance. Rooted in indigenous worldviews and ecological philosophy, RoN has gained increasing traction in both academic debates and legal frameworks worldwide (Taekema, 2021).

One of the most significant milestones in the institutionalization of RoN occurred in Ecuador's 2008 Constitution, which explicitly recognized the rights of *Pachamama* (Mother Earth) to exist and maintain its ecological cycles. This legal innovation has provided communities with the ability to sue on behalf of ecosystems, leading to landmark court rulings protecting rivers and forests from destructive development projects. Similarly, Bolivia's Law of the Rights of Mother Earth (2010) enshrined nature's rights at the national level, framing ecosystems as legal entities rather than mere resources. These Latin American cases represent pioneering attempts to embed RoN into constitutional and statutory law, transforming the relationship between state, society, and environment (Villavicencio Calzadilla, 2021).

Beyond Latin America, New Zealand has advanced the RoN discourse by granting legal personhood to natural entities. The Whanganui River, for instance, was recognized in 2017 as a legal person with its own rights, managed by both Māori representatives and the government. This recognition was grounded in indigenous Māori cosmology, which views humans and rivers as part of a shared kinship system. Similar approaches have been adopted in relation to New Zealand's Mount Taranaki and Te Urewera forests. These cases demonstrate how RoN can be adapted within diverse legal systems by incorporating cultural traditions and indigenous worldviews, bridging normative ethics and practical governance (Leal Filho et al., 2023).

Globally, RoN has sparked intense academic and policy debates. Advocates argue that granting rights to ecosystems is essential for addressing the root causes of environmental degradation, which stem from treating nature as property. RoN frameworks, they contend, provide stronger protection than conventional environmental laws, which often prioritize economic interests. Critics, however, caution that RoN can be vague, difficult to implement, and potentially in conflict with existing property rights or development goals. Some also argue that without robust enforcement mechanisms, RoN risks becoming symbolic rather than transformative. These debates highlight both the promise and the challenges of operationalizing RoN in practice (Kurbiyanto et al., 2024).

Despite these challenges, RoN has gained recognition in international forums. The United Nations has hosted multiple discussions on the concept under the banner of "Harmony with Nature," while the International Union for Conservation of Nature (IUCN) has supported the integration of RoN principles into global conservation strategies. Moreover, several jurisdictions in India, Colombia, and the United States have adopted local-level RoN ordinances, further diversifying the global landscape of RoN experiments. Together, these developments illustrate that RoN is not a marginal idea but a growing global movement, reshaping environmental governance in ways that could inspire new approaches in contexts such as Iran (Abouei & Tavasoli, 2024).

4.4 Applying RoN to Tourism in Forests

The application of the Rights of Nature (RoN) to tourism in Iran's forests requires a paradigm shift from viewing forests as recreational backdrops to recognizing them as rights-bearing entities. Under this framework, forests are not merely managed for human enjoyment but are safeguarded as subjects with the right to exist, regenerate, and thrive. This means that tourism development must operate within strict ecological thresholds, respecting the rights of forests to remain ecologically intact. Activities that compromise the integrity of ecosystems such as mass villa construction, off-road driving, or waste dumping would be seen not only as regulatory violations but also as infringements on the rights of nature (Hosseini et al., 2025).

One practical implication of adopting RoN is the establishment of visitor limits and zoning systems in forested areas. For instance, the Hyrcanian forests, currently overwhelmed by mass domestic tourism, could implement carrying-capacity assessments to determine sustainable visitor numbers. Certain zones could be designated for low-impact tourism, such as guided walks and educational tours, while other zones would be strictly off-limits to protect sensitive habitats. In the Zagros, pastoralist migration routes could be recognized as ecological corridors, with tourism activities restricted to areas where they do not interfere with forest regeneration. By adopting zoning aligned with RoN principles, Iran could prevent the overexploitation of fragile ecosystems while still allowing for sustainable tourism development (Nasirian & Naddafi, 2025).

Another application lies in eco-certification and tourism standards that explicitly integrate RoN principles. Resorts, eco-lodges, and tour operators could be required to comply with criteria ensuring minimal ecological disturbance, responsible waste management, and contributions to conservation. Certification systems could be monitored by both government agencies and community organizations, ensuring accountability at multiple levels. For example, boat tours in the Hara mangroves could be certified only if they follow wildlife-sensitive guidelines, such as restricting access during nesting seasons. This would ensure that tourism contributes to, rather than undermines, the ecological rights of mangrove ecosystems (Nathaniel & Adedoyin, 2022).

The RoN framework also has implications for legal accountability in tourism. If forests are recognized as rights-bearing entities, legal actions could be brought against tourism projects that violate those rights. This approach has precedent: in Ecuador and Colombia, rivers and forests have been plaintiffs in court cases challenging destructive practices. In Iran, similar legal innovations could empower civil society, NGOs, and communities to hold tourism operators accountable when they infringe upon the ecological integrity of forests. Such accountability would elevate conservation from a matter of policy preference to a matter of enforceable rights (O'Reilly, 2020).

Applying RoN to tourism also provides an opportunity to reframe tourism as an ally of conservation rather than a threat. By designing tourism experiences that highlight the rights and intrinsic value of forests, visitors can become participants in ecological stewardship. Educational programs, interpretive signage, and community-led ecotourism initiatives could embed RoN principles into the visitor experience. For example, in the Hyrcanian forests, tourists could learn about the forests' rights as a UNESCO World Heritage ecosystem, while in the Zagros, tribal guides could emphasize their role as custodians of both culture and nature. In this way, tourism could serve not only as an economic driver but also as a medium for spreading the ethical foundations of RoN across Iranian society (Sengar & Shah, 2025).

4.5 Community Participation and RoN in Practice

Community participation is a cornerstone of effective environmental governance, and within the Rights of Nature (RoN) framework, it becomes even more essential. If forests are recognized as rights-bearing entities, then local communities those most intimately connected to these ecosystems are natural custodians responsible for upholding those rights. This perspective reframes communities not as passive beneficiaries of conservation but as active partners in ensuring that forests can exercise their rights to exist and regenerate. In Iran, where pastoralist, tribal, and rural groups have long histories of ecological stewardship, RoN provides a normative justification for re-empowering communities as key actors in forest governance (Cheer et al., 2019).

Historically, Iranian communities practiced forms of indigenous ecological governance that align with RoN principles. In the Zagros, tribal groups such as the Bakhtiari and Qashqai managed oak woodlands through customary grazing practices, guided by seasonal rhythms that allowed forests to regenerate. In Arasbaran, Azerbaijani villagers followed taboos against cutting sacred trees or overharvesting fruits, reflecting a cultural respect for ecological limits. Fishing households in the Persian Gulf similarly developed practices for sustainable mangrove use, balancing livelihood needs with ecosystem health. These traditions, though weakened by modernization and centralized state control, demonstrate that RoN is not foreign to Iran but deeply compatible with its cultural and ecological history (Bhammar et al., 2021).

In practice, community-based tourism offers one of the most effective ways to operationalize RoN in Iran's forest regions. By placing local communities at the center of tourism development, eco-cultural tourism initiatives can ensure that economic benefits align with ecological stewardship. For example, in the Zagros, tribal communities could manage eco-lodges and guided migration tours, reinforcing both cultural traditions and ecological respect. In the Hyrcanian forests, cooperatives could lead waste management and visitor education campaigns, framing these efforts as upholding the forests' rights. In the Hara mangroves, fisher households could control boat tours, ensuring they respect wildlife habitats. Such initiatives make RoN tangible, embedding rights-based governance in everyday tourism practices (Massenberg et al., 2023).

Community participation also enhances governance legitimacy and enforcement. National institutions often struggle with enforcement due to limited resources, corruption, and political constraints. By contrast, communities possess intimate ecological knowledge and strong incentives to protect the ecosystems upon which their livelihoods depend. Under a RoN framework, communities could be legally recognized as guardians or trustees of forests, with the authority to monitor tourism activities and report violations. International cases, such as New Zealand's Whanganui River guardianship shared between Māori and government representatives, show how power-sharing models can successfully balance local traditions with state authority. Iran could adapt similar models, empowering communities as co-managers of forest heritage (Løland & Akman, 2025).

Finally, embedding RoN into community participation offers a way to integrate cultural identity with conservation ethics. Forests are not only ecological systems but also cultural landscapes that sustain songs, stories, rituals, and livelihoods. By recognizing forests as rights-bearing entities and communities as their guardians, Iran could create a governance model where ecological stewardship and cultural vitality reinforce one another. This would help counter the commodification of traditions under mass tourism, replacing it with authentic, community-led narratives of conservation. In this way, community participation is not merely a practical mechanism but a cultural and ethical bridge, ensuring that RoN principles take root in the lived realities of Iran's forest regions (Ernst et al., 2025).

4.6 Strategic Roadmap for Iran: Policy and Ethical Frameworks

The adoption of a Rights of Nature (RoN) framework in Iran requires a phased approach that balances immediate needs with long-term institutional transformation. A strategic roadmap should integrate practical policy reforms with ethical principles drawn from both global RoN discourses and Islamic stewardship traditions. By combining these dimensions, Iran can gradually shift from resource-centered governance to a holistic system that respects forests as rights-bearing entities while ensuring that tourism, livelihoods, and conservation coexist sustainably (Ghaderi et al., 2025).

In the short term, priority should be given to addressing visible and urgent ecological pressures in forest tourism. This includes implementing strict waste management systems in heavily visited sites such as the Hyrcanian forests, establishing visitor limits during peak holiday seasons, and enforcing existing bans on illegal villa construction. Educational campaigns should be launched to inform tourists that forests are not disposable recreational spaces but fragile ecosystems with intrinsic value. Even without legal recognition of RoN, these actions would reflect its principles by prioritizing ecological rights over unrestricted human use (Hariram et al., 2023).

The medium-term strategy should focus on building institutional and community capacity for participatory governance. This includes legally recognizing local communities as guardians or trustees of forest ecosystems, with authority to co-manage tourism activities and monitor ecological impacts. Ecotourism certification systems could be developed to ensure that tourism operators comply with rights-based standards, including waste reduction, habitat protection, and cultural authenticity. National policies should also be aligned with Iran's international obligations under the Convention on Biological Diversity (CBD) and UNESCO, ensuring that global recognition of forests translates into stronger domestic conservation practices (Jagielska-Burduk et al., 2021).

In the long term, Iran should pursue the formal integration of RoN into legal and policy frameworks. This could take the form of constitutional recognition of nature's rights, as in Ecuador, or statutory laws granting legal personhood to specific ecosystems, as in New Zealand. For example, the Hyrcanian forests could be recognized as a legal entity with rights to protection and regeneration, represented by a council of guardians drawn from both state institutions and local communities. Such reforms would institutionalize the principle that forests are not merely resources but subjects of rights, fundamentally reshaping the legal foundations of environmental governance in Iran (Karataş et al., 2025).

A complementary long-term priority is embedding climate resilience and adaptation strategies into forest governance. Forests are among Iran's most effective defenses against climate change impacts, including drought, floods, and desertification. By recognizing forests as rights-bearing entities, climate adaptation policies could prioritize their conservation as a moral and legal obligation, not just a technical measure. Reforestation programs, watershed restoration, and mangrove protection could thus be reframed as fulfilling the ecological rights of forests to regenerate and sustain life, aligning climate adaptation with RoN principles (Melaku & Pastor Ivars, 2024).

Finally, the strategic roadmap must emphasize the ethical dimension of governance. RoN should not be reduced to a set of legal instruments but embraced as a cultural and moral framework consistent with Islamic stewardship. By framing conservation as a duty of khalifa (stewardship) and protection of forests as prevention of fasad (corruption), Iran can ground RoN in local values, ensuring both legitimacy and compliance. In this way, Iran can pioneer a model where global environmental discourses are harmonized with cultural and religious traditions, producing a governance system that is both innovative and authentic. Such a roadmap would not only safeguard Iran's forests but also position the country as a leader in rights-based environmental governance within the Middle East and beyond.

4.7 Conclusion

Iran's forests, as explored in previous chapters, are under mounting pressure from deforestation, tourism, and climate change. Existing governance structures, though well-intentioned, remain fragmented, reactive, and weak in enforcement. The persistence of illegal villa construction in the Hyrcanian forests, oak dieback in the Zagros, and mangrove degradation in the Persian Gulf all underscore the limitations of current frameworks. If Iran is to preserve its forest heritage, a new paradigm is required one that transcends resource management and recognizes forests as living entities with intrinsic rights. The Rights of Nature (RoN) provides such a paradigm, offering both a normative foundation and a practical roadmap for integrated governance.

The adoption of RoN in Iran would not occur in a cultural vacuum. On the contrary, it resonates strongly with Islamic principles of stewardship (khalifa), trusteeship (amanat), and balance (mizan), which already view humans as caretakers rather than owners of creation. This ethical compatibility provides a culturally legitimate foundation for embedding RoN into governance, avoiding the perception of foreign imposition. By framing conservation as both a moral duty and a legal obligation, Iran could mobilize religious values alongside modern legal frameworks to strengthen ecological protection. Such a synthesis would ensure that RoN is not only legally enforceable but also socially embraced.

Practically, integrating RoN into forest tourism governance offers a pathway to transform tourism from a threat into an ally of conservation. Visitor limits, zoning, eco-certification, and community-based tourism initiatives could all be designed to uphold the rights of forests to exist and regenerate. This approach reframes tourism not merely as an economic activity but as a vehicle for ecological stewardship and cultural authenticity. By embedding RoN into tourism practices, Iran could develop a model where economic benefits, ecological protection, and cultural vitality reinforce one another, rather than compete.

Equally important is the role of community participation in operationalizing RoN. Local and tribal communities have long histories of ecological stewardship, and their inclusion as guardians or trustees of forests would ensure that governance is grounded in lived knowledge and cultural traditions. Empowering communities as co-managers alongside state institutions could bridge governance gaps, increase compliance, and enhance legitimacy. In this sense, RoN provides not only a legal and ethical framework but also a practical mechanism for participatory governance, aligning ecological sustainability with social justice.

In conclusion, Iran's forests stand at a crossroads between continued degradation and transformative renewal. By adopting an integrated governance model rooted in the Rights of Nature, Iran has the opportunity to safeguard its forest heritage for future generations. Such a model would align national policies with global sustainability agendas, strengthen climate resilience, and harmonize international discourses with Islamic stewardship traditions. Ultimately, RoN offers more than a legal innovation—it provides a holistic vision of forests as living heritage, where ecology, culture, and ethics converge. Embracing this framework could position Iran not only as a steward of its own forests but also as a pioneer of rights-based environmental governance in the region and the world.

CHAPTER 5

PATHWAYS TOWARD SUSTAINABLE TOURISM IN IRANIAN HERITAGE FORESTS

5.1 Introduction: From Challenges to Opportunities

Iran's heritage forests stand at a critical turning point. As previous chapters have shown, ecosystems such as the Hyrcanian, Zagros, Arasbaran, and Hara mangroves are globally significant for their biodiversity, cultural traditions, and ecological services. Yet, they are under severe pressure from deforestation, illegal construction, overgrazing, climate change, and unregulated tourism. Current governance frameworks, while extensive on paper, remain fragmented and weak in enforcement. The persistence of degradation despite decades of policy reform demonstrates that incremental adjustments to the status quo are insufficient. What is required is a paradigm shift in how tourism and forests are conceptualized, governed, and practiced (Sobhani et al., 2025).

Tourism, as discussed in Chapter 3, embodies a duality: it is both a threat and an opportunity for forests. When unmanaged, tourism accelerates waste accumulation, habitat fragmentation, and cultural commodification. But when managed within ecological thresholds, it can generate revenue for conservation, strengthen community livelihoods, and increase environmental awareness among visitors. This dual nature means that tourism must be strategically directed rather than simply expanded. For Iran, the challenge is not whether tourism should grow in heritage forests, but how it can evolve into a force that sustains rather than depletes ecological and cultural systems (Asadi et al., 2022).

The concept of sustainability provides a guiding framework for this evolution. Sustainable tourism is not about freezing development but about aligning visitor activities with ecological capacity, cultural integrity, and community well-being. This requires a balance between ecological protection, cultural authenticity, and economic viability. In forest contexts, sustainability means limiting visitor numbers to carrying capacity, embedding education into tourism experiences, and ensuring that revenues are reinvested into conservation and local development. In this way, tourism becomes a tool for ecological stewardship and cultural continuity rather than a driver of degradation (Bhammar et al., 2021).

Opportunities for sustainable tourism in Iran's forests are considerable. The Hyrcanian forests, with their UNESCO World Heritage recognition, could serve as models of ecotourism if managed with strict conservation standards. The Zagros forests, with their tribal heritage, could host eco-cultural tourism that strengthens both ecological stewardship and cultural identity. Arasbaran and the Hara mangroves, while ecologically fragile, could attract niche markets for birdwatching, education, and community-led tours. International experiences demonstrate that when communities are empowered and governance is strengthened, forest tourism can simultaneously support biodiversity, cultural resilience, and economic diversification (Bui et al., 2020).

This chapter explores the pathways toward sustainable tourism in Iranian heritage forests. It begins by outlining the principles of sustainability in forest ecosystems before examining how tourism can be integrated with conservation goals. It then considers the role of community-led models, policy frameworks, and technological innovations in shaping sustainable practices. Finally, it presents a strategic roadmap that links short-term actions with long-term structural reforms, including the integration of the Rights of Nature framework. In doing so, the chapter reframes Iran's heritage forests not as victims of tourism but as living landscapes where tourism, culture, and ecology can reinforce one another.

5.2 Principles of Sustainable Tourism in Forest Ecosystems

The first principle of sustainable tourism in forest ecosystems is the recognition of ecological thresholds and carrying capacity. Forests have finite resilience, and exceeding these thresholds results in irreversible degradation. In Iran, the Hyrcanian forests already experience ecological stress during holiday seasons, when visitor numbers far surpass what the ecosystem can absorb. Soil compaction, littering, and vegetation loss are direct outcomes of unchecked visitation. A sustainable approach requires careful assessment of carrying capacity, coupled with zoning systems that designate areas for tourism, conservation, and restricted use. By respecting ecological limits, tourism can operate without undermining the very ecosystems that attract visitors (Paing et al., 2022).

The second principle is the preservation of cultural integrity and authenticity. Forests are not only ecological spaces but also cultural landscapes where traditions, rituals, and livelihoods are deeply embedded. In the Zagros and Arasbaran regions, tribal communities maintain ecological knowledge and cultural practices that are integral to heritage tourism. However, unregulated tourism risks commodifying these traditions, turning them into performances tailored to visitor demand. Sustainable tourism must therefore ensure that cultural practices are presented on community terms, reinforcing rather than eroding authenticity. Cultural sustainability is achieved when tourism strengthens identity, intergenerational knowledge transfer, and pride in local heritage (Sharma, 2025).

The third principle concerns economic viability and equity. For tourism to be sustainable, it must generate benefits that are both long-term and fairly distributed. In Iran, the economic benefits of tourism often concentrate among wealthier households or private investors, while rural communities face the costs of ecological degradation. Sustainable tourism requires revenue-sharing mechanisms that ensure communities receive direct financial benefits, whether through employment, cooperative ownership of eco-lodges, or royalties from entrance fees. Equitable distribution reduces social tensions and incentivizes communities to engage in conservation as a shared responsibility (Khater et al., 2024).

A fourth principle involves the integration of education and environmental awareness into tourism practices. Visitors often underestimate the fragility of forest ecosystems, treating them as limitless recreational spaces. By embedding education into tourism through guided tours, interpretive centers, and signage forests can become classrooms that cultivate ecological responsibility. For example, visitors to the Hara mangroves could learn about the ecological role of mangroves in carbon storage and coastal protection, transforming recreational visits into opportunities for environmental learning. Education strengthens the cultural shift needed for sustainability, where forests are respected as rights-bearing ecosystems rather than exploited resources (Ansari et al., 2023).

Finally, sustainable tourism must be anchored in long-term resilience and adaptability. Forest ecosystems are dynamic, subject to pressures from climate change, pests, and human activity. Tourism systems must therefore be flexible, capable of adapting to new ecological realities. This may include adjusting visitor limits during drought years, shifting tourism activities to less vulnerable sites, or integrating new technologies for monitoring and management. By embedding adaptability into tourism planning, Iran can ensure that forest tourism contributes not only to short-term benefits but also to the long-term resilience of both ecosystems and communities.

5.3   Integrating Sustainable Tourism with Conservation Goals

Sustainable tourism in forest ecosystems must go beyond minimizing harm; it should actively contribute to conservation outcomes. This requires aligning tourism practices with biodiversity protection, restoration initiatives, and ecological monitoring. In Iran, where forests face pressures from illegal logging, overgrazing, and climate change, tourism revenues and visitor engagement can be redirected toward ecological protection. When designed within a conservation framework, tourism becomes not only compatible with heritage preservation but also a driver of environmental stewardship (N. Khan et al., 2020).

A key mechanism for integration is the reinvestment of tourism revenues into conservation. Entrance fees, eco-lodge profits, and guided tour charges can be partially earmarked for forest management, habitat restoration, and wildlife protection. For instance, revenues generated in the Hyrcanian forests could fund anti-logging patrols and waste management systems, while in the Zagros, tourism income could support oak regeneration projects and pest control efforts. International examples, such as Costa Rica's national park funding model, demonstrate that when revenues are transparently reinvested, tourism creates a positive feedback loop where visitors directly contribute to ecosystem resilience (Nathaniel & Adedoyin, 2022).

Another pathway lies in embedding conservation education into the visitor experience. Tourists often underestimate their ecological footprint, engaging in practices that unintentionally harm forests. By integrating guided tours, interpretive signage, and participatory workshops, tourism can cultivate ecological awareness. In the Hara mangroves, for example, boat tours could include educational briefings about migratory bird habitats and mangrove carbon storage functions. In Arasbaran, visitors could learn from local communities about traditional ecological knowledge. Such initiatives transform tourism into an educational tool, fostering long-term support for conservation among both domestic and international visitors (Ghaderi et al., 2025).

Tourism can also contribute to biodiversity monitoring and research. Citizen science initiatives such as birdwatching records, wildlife photography, or participatory biodiversity surveys can supplement scientific data while engaging visitors in conservation activities. This approach has been successfully implemented in several ecotourism destinations worldwide and could be adapted to Iran's forests, particularly in biodiversity hotspots like the Hyrcanian and Arasbaran. By turning visitors into active participants in ecological monitoring, tourism can help generate the data needed for adaptive management while cultivating a sense of responsibility toward forest ecosystems (Jong, 2024).

Ultimately, integrating tourism with conservation requires a paradigm shift in governance and planning. Instead of treating tourism and conservation as separate or competing domains, policies must design tourism as a conservation strategy in itself. This involves establishing partnerships between government agencies, local communities, and private operators, ensuring that conservation is embedded in every stage of tourism development. In this way, Iran's heritage forests can become models of sustainable tourism where biodiversity protection, cultural preservation, and economic development reinforce one another (Iskakova et al., 2021; Jagielska-Burduk et al., 2021).

5.4 Community-Led Tourism Models

Community-led tourism represents one of the most effective pathways for achieving sustainability in heritage forests. Unlike top-down tourism development, which often prioritizes external investors and mass infrastructure, community-led models place local people at the center of decision-making, ownership, and benefit-sharing. For Iran, where tribal and rural communities have historically acted as custodians of forests, this approach is both culturally authentic and economically equitable. By empowering communities as managers rather than marginal participants, tourism can become a tool for strengthening ecological stewardship while preserving cultural heritage (Fairclough, 2019).

In the Zagros forests, tribal groups such as the Bakhtiari, Qashqai, and Kurdish communities embody traditions that can be integrated into eco-cultural tourism. Seasonal migrations, music, handicrafts, and pastoralist knowledge offer unique cultural experiences for visitors. Community-led tourism could allow tribes to design and manage such experiences on their own terms, ensuring that cultural practices are celebrated rather than commodified. Revenues could support both livelihoods and conservation, reducing reliance on extractive practices such as overgrazing or firewood collection. In this way, eco-cultural tourism reinforces ecological and cultural sustainability simultaneously (Ansari et al., 2023).

The Hyrcanian forests provide opportunities for cooperatives and village-based initiatives. Communities could manage eco-lodges, camping areas, and guided forest tours, embedding environmental education and conservation practices into visitor experiences. Local cooperatives could also oversee waste management and reforestation projects, directly linking tourism income to ecosystem health. This approach would counteract the negative impacts of mass villa construction by offering alternative, community-owned accommodation options. It would also shift tourism development away from private speculation and toward collective stewardship of forest resources (Leal Filho et al., 2023).

The Hara mangroves highlight the role of coastal and fishing communities in community-based tourism. Boat tours, birdwatching activities, and mangrove education programs could be managed by local households rather than external operators. Revenues would then support both livelihoods and mangrove protection, creating strong incentives for conservation. Similar models in Southeast Asia show that when fishing communities manage ecotourism, they are more likely to regulate boat traffic, control visitor numbers, and protect wildlife habitats. Applying this model to Qeshm Island could transform ecotourism into a driver of coastal stewardship, ensuring that mangroves are respected as rights-bearing ecosystems (N. Khan et al., 2020).

International experiences reinforce the potential of community-led models. From Nepal's Annapurna Conservation Area to Costa Rica's community-based ecotourism cooperatives, evidence shows that when communities are empowered with ownership and responsibility, conservation outcomes improve while economic benefits are distributed more fairly. For Iran, adopting such models would require legal recognition of community rights, training in sustainable tourism management, and access to markets. Yet the rewards are significant: stronger governance, cultural continuity, and ecological resilience. By positioning communities as the primary agents of tourism, Iran can align heritage preservation with local empowerment, ensuring that sustainable tourism is both socially inclusive and ecologically effective (Paing et al., 2022).

5.5 Policy and Governance for Sustainable Forest Tourism

The success of sustainable tourism in Iran's forests ultimately depends on the strength of governance systems that regulate development and protect ecosystems. While community-led initiatives and local traditions play vital roles, they require supportive policies and institutional frameworks to thrive. Current governance in Iran remains fragmented, with the Forests, Range and Watershed Management Organization (FRWO), the Department of Environment (DoE), and the Ministry of Cultural Heritage, Tourism and Handicrafts working in parallel but often at cross-purposes. A coherent governance model must integrate these institutions under a shared vision that explicitly links tourism development to ecological sustainability. Without such coordination, policies risk remaining symbolic rather than transformative (Madani et al., 2024).

Enforcement of existing laws is a critical starting point. Despite bans on logging and restrictions on villa construction in forest zones, illegal development continues to spread in regions such as Mazandaran and Gilan. Weak enforcement, limited monitoring capacity, and corruption undermine conservation efforts and embolden violators. A sustainable governance framework must therefore prioritize enforcement through stronger monitoring systems, increased penalties for violations, and transparent accountability mechanisms. Investment in ranger programs, satellite surveillance, and judicial reforms could significantly enhance enforcement capacity, ensuring that tourism development respects ecological and legal boundaries (Nasirian & Naddafi, 2025).

At the same time, governance must embrace integrated land-use planning that balances tourism with conservation priorities. This means designating forest areas for strict protection, controlled tourism, and community-based development, guided by scientific assessments of ecological thresholds. Land-use zoning should also take into account tribal migration routes, local livelihoods, and climate adaptation needs. Such integration would prevent the unchecked sprawl of villas and resorts, replacing ad hoc development with systematic planning. Impocontext sensitive planning should involve local communities in decision-making, ensuring that governance is both participatory and context-sensitive (Madani et al., 2024).

Eco-certification and sustainability standards represent another key governance tool. Tourism operators, including eco-lodges, resorts, and tour companies, should be required to comply with certification criteria that address waste management, energy use, cultural authenticity, and biodiversity protection. Certification schemes could be developed in partnership with NGOs and international organizations, drawing on models from Costa Rica or the European Union. Certified operators would not only ensure ecological responsibility but also gain competitive advantage in international markets, attracting tourists who seek authentic and sustainable experiences. By institutionalizing eco-certification, governance frameworks can align private-sector incentives with conservation goals (Paing et al., 2022).

Finally, governance reform must be anchored in a multi-level approach that connects local, national, and international frameworks. At the local level, communities should be empowered as co-managers of forest tourism. At the national level, policies must integrate FRWO, DoE, and tourism mandates into a unified system. At the international level, Iran should align its governance with obligations under UNESCO, the Convention on Biological Diversity (CBD), and the Sustainable Development Goals (SDGs). This multi-level governance model would ensure coherence across scales, embedding sustainable tourism within a broader framework of ecological protection and global responsibility.

By pursuing such reforms, Iran can move beyond fragmented policies to establish a robust governance system capable of safeguarding its forest heritage.

5.6 Innovation and Technology in Forest Tourism

Innovation and technology can play a transformative role in advancing sustainable forest tourism in Iran. Traditional approaches to tourism management have often relied on limited human monitoring and reactive policies, leaving ecosystems vulnerable to overuse and degradation. By integrating digital tools, renewable energy systems, and innovative educational platforms, Iran can modernize its tourism sector while aligning it with sustainability goals. These technologies not only enhance efficiency but also increase transparency, accountability, and visitor engagement, ensuring that tourism supports rather than undermines ecological resilience (Skrimizea & Parra, 2019).

One of the most promising applications is the use of digital monitoring systems to regulate visitor flows and track ecological impacts. Geographic Information Systems (GIS), drones, and satellite imagery can be deployed to map tourist hotspots, monitor illegal land use, and assess forest health in real time. Mobile applications could provide tourists with information about permitted areas while also collecting data on visitor numbers and behaviors. For example, a digital entry system in the Hyrcanian forests could automatically limit access once carrying capacity is reached, ensuring ecological thresholds are respected. These tools create a feedback loop between monitoring, policy enforcement, and sustainable visitor management (Karataş et al., 2025).

Renewable energy technologies can also reduce the ecological footprint of tourism infrastructure. Eco-lodges and visitor centers in forests could be powered by solar panels, biogas systems, or small-scale wind turbines, minimizing reliance on fossil fuels. Water-saving technologies, such as rainwater harvesting and greywater recycling, could reduce pressure on local water resources, especially in semi-arid regions of the Zagros. These innovations not only decrease environmental impacts but also showcase forests as spaces for sustainable living, providing educational examples for visitors and local communities alike (Mandić et al., 2025).

Digital platforms also offer opportunities for virtual and augmented reality experiences, which can reduce physical pressures on fragile ecosystems while enhancing visitor education. For example, virtual tours of the Hara mangroves could allow tourists to experience biodiversity without disturbing nesting birds. Augmented reality in the Hyrcanian forests could overlay historical and ecological information onto landscapes during guided walks, deepening visitor engagement without increasing environmental strain. Such technologies expand access to heritage forests while minimizing physical impacts, creating a balance between conservation and experiential tourism (Wani et al., 2025).

Finally, innovation must be embedded in a broader strategy of inclusive and adaptive governance. Technology should not be seen as a substitute for community participation but as a tool that empowers both communities and institutions. For instance, mobile apps could allow local residents to report illegal logging or waste dumping, integrating traditional stewardship with modern surveillance. Similarly, eco-certification programs could use blockchain technology to ensure transparency in revenue distribution, reinforcing trust between communities, tourists, and the state. By combining innovation with cultural and ethical frameworks, Iran can pioneer a model of forest tourism that is technologically advanced, socially inclusive, and ecologically sustainable.

5.7 Strategic Roadmap for Iran's Heritage Forests

Designing a strategic roadmap for sustainable tourism in Iran's heritage forests requires balancing immediate interventions with long-term structural reforms. Forest ecosystems are fragile and face overlapping pressures from tourism, deforestation, and climate change. Thus, strategies must be phased: short-term measures to address urgent ecological challenges, medium-term policies to build governance and community capacity, and long-term reforms to institutionalize sustainability principles. This phased approach ensures that Iran's tourism sector evolves gradually, avoiding both ecological collapse and abrupt disruptions to livelihoods (Zandebasiri et al., 2023).

In the short term, the priority should be to mitigate the most visible and damaging impacts of tourism. This includes implementing comprehensive waste management systems in the Hyrcanian forests, introducing strict visitor limits during peak holiday seasons, and designating zoning systems to separate conservation areas from recreational spaces. Awareness campaigns should educate tourists about their responsibilities in respecting fragile ecosystems, framing these actions within cultural and religious values of stewardship. Rapid-response enforcement mechanisms against illegal villa construction or off-road driving should also be established to prevent further degradation. These immediate interventions would stabilize forests while laying the foundation for more systemic reforms (Villavicencio Calzadilla, 2021).

The medium-term strategy should focus on strengthening institutional capacity and community participation. Local communities tribal groups in the Zagros, fishing households in the Hara mangroves, and rural cooperatives in the Hyrcanian region should be formally recognized as co-managers of forest tourism. This would involve training in sustainable tourism practices, financial support for eco-lodges and cooperatives, and integration into decision-making councils. At the same time, eco-certification programs should be introduced to regulate tourism operators, ensuring compliance with sustainability standards. Medium-term policies should also improve coordination between the FRWO, DoE, and the Ministry of Tourism, replacing fragmented mandates with integrated governance structures (Tehseen et al., 2024).

In the long term, Iran must institutionalize sustainability principles within its legal and policy frameworks. This could include formal recognition of Rights of Nature (RoN) for specific forest ecosystems, granting them legal personhood and enforceable rights to exist and regenerate. The Hyrcanian forests, given their UNESCO World Heritage status, could be the first candidate for such recognition, with a guardianship council representing both state and community interests. Long-term strategies should also embed climate resilience into forest tourism, ensuring that activities adapt to ecological shifts such as droughts, wildfires, and sea-level rise. By institutionalizing rights-based and climate-sensitive governance, Iran can secure the future of its heritage forests (Jagielska-Burduk et al., 2021).

Another long-term priority is the integration of innovation and technology into forest tourism systems. Digital monitoring platforms should regulate visitor flows, while renewable energy infrastructure can reduce the ecological footprint of accommodations. Virtual and augmented reality can provide alternatives to physical visitation in ecologically sensitive areas, broadening access while minimizing strain. These technologies must be deployed in ways that empower local communities, ensuring that innovation enhances rather than displaces traditional stewardship practices. By blending modern tools with cultural values, Iran can create a tourism system that is both technologically advanced and culturally rooted (Smith et al., 2023).

Ultimately, the strategic roadmap must emphasize multi-level governance and global integration. At the local level, communities should manage tourism projects and share in their benefits. At the national level, integrated policies should link conservation, tourism, and climate strategies. At the international level, Iran should leverage its UNESCO-recognized forests and CBD commitments to access funding, expertise, and partnerships. By aligning local action with national policies and global frameworks, Iran can position its forests as models of sustainable heritage tourism. This multi-scalar approach ensures resilience, legitimacy, and long-term effectiveness (Dering et al., 2021).

5.8 Conclusion

Iran's heritage forests Hyrcanian, Zagros, Arasbaran, and the Hara mangroves represent ecological treasures of global significance and cultural landscapes of deep national identity. Yet, as demonstrated throughout this book, these ecosystems face mounting threats from deforestation, unregulated tourism, climate change, and weak governance. Despite policy reforms, forest degradation continues, showing that incremental adjustments to existing frameworks are inadequate. A transition toward sustainable tourism is not an option but a necessity if Iran is to preserve its forests as living heritage for future generations (Croker et al., 2023).

The principles of sustainable tourism ecological thresholds, cultural authenticity, and equitable economics provide a strong foundation for this transition. Tourism must operate within the carrying capacity of forests, respect the traditions and knowledge of local communities, and distribute benefits fairly. When aligned with conservation goals, tourism can fund ecological protection, enhance biodiversity monitoring, and cultivate environmental awareness among visitors. Instead of treating tourism as a threat, Iran has the opportunity to reframe it as a strategic ally in conservation, transforming challenges into opportunities (Liburd et al., 2024).

Central to this vision is the role of communities as custodians of forests. Tribal, rural, and coastal populations have long histories of ecological stewardship, and their inclusion in governance is critical for sustainability. Community-led tourism models eco-lodges in the Hyrcanian, eco-cultural tours in the Zagros, and cooperative-managed boat tours in the Hara mangroves can ensure that cultural integrity and ecological protection reinforce one another. Empowering communities not only strengthens governance legitimacy but also ensures that economic benefits support those most closely tied to forests (Romagny et al., 2024).

The path forward also requires institutional reform and innovation. Stronger enforcement against illegal land conversion, integrated land-use planning, and eco-certification for operators are essential governance tools. Technological innovations from GIS-based monitoring to renewable energy in eco-lodges and virtual reality tours can reduce the ecological footprint of tourism while enhancing education and engagement. Long-term structural change should embed the Rights of Nature into Iran's legal frameworks, reframing forests as rights-bearing entities and ensuring their protection beyond short-term political or economic pressures (Sharma, 2025).

In conclusion, Iran's forests stand at a crossroads. They can continue to degrade under unchecked tourism and weak governance, or they can be transformed into models of sustainable heritage tourism where ecology, culture, and economy coexist in balance. By adopting a strategic roadmap grounded in sustainability principles, community participation, governance reform, and normative innovation through Rights of Nature, Iran can secure a future where its forests thrive as living heritage. This vision not only preserves national identity and ecological integrity but also positions Iran as a regional leader in sustainable forest governance and tourism. The choice today will define whether future generations inherit degraded remnants or vibrant forests that embody both natural and cultural resilience.

ABOUT THE AUTHOR

The author, Atieh Mashayekhi, is a tourism management specialist holding a Master's degree from Allameh Tabataba'i University, where her research focused on the intersection of media communication and environmental behavior in tourism. Building upon that foundational work, this book represents a comprehensive scholarly endeavor that bridges the conceptual pillars of sustainable tourism, the "Rights of Nature" framework, and the pressing environmental challenges facing Iran's heritage forests. It offers a critical examination of tourism development while proposing normative frameworks and practical pathways to balance ecological preservation with cultural heritage in these fragile ecosystems.

References

Abdelhak, M. (2022). Soil improvement in arid and semiarid regions for sustainable development. In *Natural resources conservation and advances for sustainability* (pp. 73-90). Elsevier.

Abouei, R., & Tavasoli, M. (2024). The Dilemma of Urban Heritage Conservation in Post-Conflict Bamiyan: A Critical Analysis of Causes, Failures, Consequences and Prospects. *The Historic Environment: Policy & Practice, 15*(4), 517-539.

Akalibey, S., Hlaváčková, P., Schneider, J., Fialová, J., Darkwah, S., & Ahenkan, A. (2024). Integrating indigenous knowledge and culture in sustainable forest management via global environmental policies. *Journal of Forest Science, 70*(6), 265.

Aktymbayeva, A., Nuruly, Y., Artemyev, A., Kaliyeva, A., Sapiyeva, A., & Assipova, Z. (2023). Balancing nature and visitors for sustainable development: Assessing the tourism carrying capacities of Katon-Karagay National Park, Kazakhstan. *Sustainability, 15*(22), 15989.

Amloy, A., Wonglangka, W., Ounchanum, P., Ruangwitthayanusorn, S., Siriphon, A., & Oranratmanee, R. (2024). Agroecology, tourism, and community adaptability under UNESCO biosphere reserve: A case study of smallholders in northern Thailand. *Sustainable development, 32*(5), 4428-4439.

Ansari, A., Ghorbanpour, M., Kazemi, A., & Kariman, K. (2023). Ecological assessment of Iran's terrestrial biomes for wildlife conservation. *Scientific Reports, 13*(1), 17761.

Asadi, A., Bayat, N., Zanganeh Shahraki, S., Ahmadifard, N., Poponi, S., & Salvati, L. (2022). Challenges toward sustainability? Experiences and approaches to literary tourism from Iran. *Sustainability, 14*(18), 11709.

Baloch, Q. B., Shah, S. N., Iqbal, N., Sheeraz, M., Asadullah, M., Mahar, S., & Khan, A. U. (2023). Impact of tourism development upon environmental sustainability: a suggested framework for sustainable ecotourism. *Environmental Science and Pollution Research, 30*(3), 5917-5930.

Basnyat, B., Treue, T., Pokharel, R. K., Kayastha, P. K., & Shrestha, G. K. (2023). Conservation by corruption: The hidden yet regulated economy in Nepal's community forest timber sector. *Forest Policy and Economics, 149*, 102917.

Betts, J., Young, R. P., Hilton-Taylor, C., Hoffmann, M., Rodríguez, J. P., Stuart, S. N., & Milner-Gulland, E. (2020). A framework for evaluating the impact of the IUCN Red List of threatened species. *Conservation Biology, 34*(3), 632-643.

Bhammar, H., Li, W., Molina, C. M. M., Hickey, V., Pendry, J., & Narain, U. (2021). Framework for sustainable recovery of tourism in protected areas. *Sustainability, 13*(5), 2798.

Bieling, C., Eser, U., & Plieninger, T. (2020). Towards a better understanding of values in sustainability transformations: ethical perspectives on landscape stewardship. *Ecosystems and People, 16*(1), 188-196.

Bridgewater, P., & Rotherham, I. D. (2019). A critical perspective on the concept of biocultural diversity and its emerging role in nature and heritage conservation. *People and Nature, 1*(3), 291-304.

Bui, H. T., Jones, T. E., Weaver, D. B., & Le, A. (2020). The adaptive resilience of living cultural heritage in a tourism destination. *Journal of sustainable tourism, 28*(7), 1022-1040.

Cárcamo Macoto, H. L., Viñals, M. J., & Sanders, A. (2024). Cultural Landscapes in the Central American Region: Analysis of the Legal Framework for Protection and Management. *Heritage, 7*(8), 4520-4537.

Cheer, J. M., Milano, C., & Novelli, M. (2019). Tourism and community resilience in the Anthropocene: Accentuating temporal overtourism. *Journal of sustainable tourism, 27*(4), 554-572.

Collins, A. M., Grant, J. A., & Ackah-Baidoo, P. (2019). The glocal dynamics of land reform in natural resource sectors: Insights from Tanzania. *Land Use Policy, 81*, 889-896.

Constant, N. L., & Taylor, P. J. (2020). Restoring the forest revives our culture: Ecosystem services and values for ecological restoration across the rural-urban nexus in South Africa. *Forest Policy and Economics, 118*, 102222.

Croker, A. R., Woods, J., & Kountouris, Y. (2023). Changing fire regimes in East and Southern Africa's savanna-protected areas: opportunities and challenges for indigenous-led savanna burning emissions abatement schemes. *Fire Ecology, 19*(1), 63.

Dering, M., Baranowska, M., Beridze, B., Chybicki, I., Danelia, I., Iszkuło, G., Kvartskhava, G., Kosiński, P., Rączka, G., & Thomas, P. (2021). The evolutionary heritage and ecological uniqueness of Scots pine in the Caucasus ecoregion is at risk of climate changes. *Scientific Reports, 11*(1), 22845.

Dushkova, D., & Ivlieva, O. (2024). Empowering communities to act for a change: A review of the community empowerment programs towards sustainability and resilience. *Sustainability, 16*(19), 8700.

Ernst, M., Portik, D. M., Segniagbeto, G. H., Ofori-Boateng, C., Doumbia, J., Penner, J., Kouamé, N. G. G., Fujita, M. K., Leaché, A. D., Blom, M. P. K., & Rödel, M.-O. (2025). Comparative Phylogeography of West African Rainforest Frogs Reveals Regional Variation in Refugia Dynamics. *Molecular Ecology, 34*(17), e70043. https://doi.org/https://doi.org/10.1111/mec.70043

Fairclough, G. (2019). Landscape and heritage: ideas from Europe for culturally based solutions in rural environments. *Journal of Environmental Planning and Management, 62*(7), 1149-1165.

Farina, A. (2022). Human-Dependent Landscapes Around the World–An Ecological Perspective. In *Principles and Methods in Landscape Ecology: An Agenda for the Second Millennium* (pp. 339-399). Springer.

Fayvush, G., Aghababyan, K., Aleksanyan, A., Arakelyan, M., Gasparyan, A., Kalashian, M., Margaryan, L., & Nanagulyan, S. (2023). Biodiversity Conservation Problems. In *Biodiversity of Armenia* (pp. 283-321). Springer.

Flood, K., Wilson, D., & Renou-Wilson, F. (2025). Evidence Synthesis and Knowledge Integration for Sustainable Peatland Management. *Land, 14*(7), 1397. https://www.mdpi.com/2073-445X/14/7/1397

Gaodirelwe, I., Masunga, G. S., & Motsholapheko, M. R. (2020). Community-based natural resource management: A promising strategy for reducing subsistence poaching around protected areas, northern Botswana. *Environment, Development and Sustainability, 22*(3), 2269-2287.

Ghaderi, Z., & Henderson, J. C. (2012, 2012/04/01/). Sustainable rural tourism in Iran: A perspective from Hawraman Village. *Tourism management perspectives, 2-3,* 47-54. https://doi.org/https://doi.org/10.1016/j.tmp.2012.03.001

Ghaderi, Z., Makian, S., & Kuhzady, S. (2025). Green grabbing and neofeudalism governance in ecotourism destinations: an insight from Iran. *Journal of Ecotourism*, 1-20.

Ghorbani, A., Zhu, K., Mousazadeh, H., Almani, F. A., Zangiabadi, A., Pireh, M., & Dávid, L. D. (2023). Sustainable behaviors conceptualization for Forest adventures Tours: the case of Cloud Ocean sites in Hyrcanian forests listed as UNESCO's world heritage property. *Forests, 14*(5), 1034.

Goushehgir, Z., Feghhi, J., & Innes, J. L. (2022). Challenges facing the improvement of forest management in the Hyrcanian forests of Iran. *Forests, 13*(12), 2180.

Haq, S. M., Pieroni, A., Bussmann, R. W., Abd-ElGawad, A. M., & El-Ansary, H. O. (2023). Integrating traditional ecological knowledge into habitat restoration: implications for meeting forest restoration challenges. *Journal of Ethnobiology and Ethnomedicine, 19*(1), 33.

Hariram, N., Mekha, K., Suganthan, V., & Sudhakar, K. (2023). Sustainalism: An integrated socio-economic-environmental model to address sustainable development and sustainability. *Sustainability, 15*(13), 10682.

Haseeba, K. P., Aboobacker, V. M., Vethamony, P., & Al-Khayat, J. A. (2025). Significance of Avicennia Marina in the Arabian Gulf environment: A review. *Wetlands, 45*(1), 16.

Hosseini, S., Amirnejad, H., & Azadi, H. (2025). Impacts of Hyrcanian forest ecosystem loss: the case of Northern Iran. *Environment, Development and Sustainability, 27*(6), 14397-14418.

Iskakova, K., Bayandinova, S., Aliyeva, Z., Aktymbayeva, A., & Baiburiyev, R. (2021). Ecological Tourism in the Republic of Kazakhstan.

Jagielska-Burduk, A., Pszczyński, M., & Stec, P. (2021). Cultural heritage education in UNESCO cultural conventions. *Sustainability, 13*(6), 3548.

Jain, S., Srivastava, A., Khadke, L., Chatterjee, U., & Elbeltagi, A. (2024). Global-scale water security and desertification management amidst climate change. *Environmental Science and Pollution Research, 31*(49), 58720-58744.

Tourism, Heritage Forests, and the Rights of Nature: Pathways to Sustainable
Development in Iran

Janzen, D. H., & Hallwachs, W. (2020). Área de Conservación Guanacaste, northwestern Costa Rica: Converting a tropical national park to conservation via biodevelopment. *Biotropica, 52*(6), 1017-1029.

Jong, A. (2024). Social theory and navigating indeterminacy: a configurational analysis of Iranian youth's identity construction in contemporary Iran. *Societies, 14*(3), 32.

Karataş, E., Özköse, A., & Heyik, M. A. (2025). Sustainable Heritage Planning for Urban Mass Tourism and Rural Abandonment: An Integrated Approach to the Safranbolu–Amasra Eco-Cultural Route. *Sustainability (2071-1050), 17*(7).

Karimi, A., Yazdandad, H., & Reside, A. E. (2023). Spatial conservation prioritization for locating protected area gaps in Iran. *Biological Conservation, 279*, 109902.

Khan, A., Bibi, S., Ardito, L., Lyu, J., Hayat, H., & Arif, A. M. (2020). Revisiting the dynamics of tourism, economic growth, and environmental pollutants in the emerging economies—sustainable tourism policy implications. *Sustainability, 12*(6), 2533.

Khan, N., Hassan, A. U., Fahad, S., & Naushad, M. (2020). Factors affecting tourism industry and its impacts on global economy of the world. *Available at SSRN 3559353*.

Khater, M., Ibrahim, O., Sayed, M. N. E., & Faik, M. (2024). Legal frameworks for sustainable tourism: Balancing environmental conservation and economic development. *Current Issues in Tourism*, 1-22.

Khosravi Mashizi, A., & Sharafatmandrad, M. (2023). Cultural services in arid landscapes. A comparative study based on people's perception, southeast of Iran. *Arid land research and management, 37*(4), 619-636.

Koot, S. (2019). Autoethnography and power in a tourism researcher position: A self-reflexive exploration of unawareness, memories and paternalism among Namibian Bushmen 1. In *Tourism Ethnographies* (pp. 52-66). Routledge.

Kurbiyanto, A., Yusmaliana, D., Fitriana, F., Altiarika, E., & Sabri, F. (2024). Environmental Ethics in Islamic Teachings: Discussing Ethical Principles in Islamic Teachings that Emphasize Environmental Protection and Preservation. In *Navigating Peace and Sustainability in an Increasingly Complex World* (pp. 15-34). Springer.

Lachs, L., & Oñate-Casado, J. (2020). Fisheries and tourism: Social, economic, and ecological trade-offs in coral reef systems. In *Youmares 9-the oceans: Our research, our future* (pp. 243-260). Springer, Cham.

Leal Filho, W., Ng, A. W., Sharifi, A., Janová, J., Özuyar, P. G., Hemani, C., Heyes, G., Njau, D., & Rampasso, I. (2023). Global tourism, climate change and energy sustainability: assessing carbon reduction mitigating measures from the aviation industry. *Sustainability Science, 18*(2), 983-996.

Liburd, J., Menke, B., & Tomej, K. (2024). Activating socio-cultural values for sustainable tourism development in natural protected areas. *Journal of sustainable tourism, 32*(6), 1182-1200.

Liburd, J. J., & Becken, S. (2020). Values in nature conservation, tourism and UNESCO World Heritage Site stewardship. In *Protected areas, sustainable tourism and neo-liberal governance policies* (pp. 23-39). Routledge.

Løland, I., & Akman, H. (2025). Echoes of the mountain: exploring biocultural diversity and transformative learning within the storied landscape of Kurdish tradition. *Intercultural Education*, 1-17.

Madani, J., Nemati, V., Mostafazadeh, R., & Ashja, H. (2024). Factors influencing and controlling vandalism by tourists and local indigenous communities at the Fandoghlou forest natural site. *Journal of Outdoor Recreation and Tourism, 48*, 100830.

Mandić, A., Birendra, K., Bricker, K. S., & Novaković, M. (2025). GSTC evaluation of urban and nature-based tourism destinations in Croatia: implications for adaptive governance and resilience. *Journal of Ecotourism*, 1-22.

Markley, P. T., Gross, C. P., & Daru, B. H. (2025). The changing biodiversity of the Arctic flora in the Anthropocene. *American Journal of Botany, 112*(2), e16466. https://doi.org/https://doi.org/10.1002/ajb2.16466

Massenberg, J. R., Schiller, J., & Schröter-Schlaack, C. (2023). Towards a holistic approach to rewilding in cultural landscapes. *People and Nature, 5*(1), 45-56.

Mehri, S., Alesheikh, A. A., & Lotfata, A. (2024, 2024/02/17). Abiotic factors impact on oak forest decline in Lorestan Province, Western Iran. *Scientific Reports,* *14*(1), 3973. https://doi.org/10.1038/s41598-024-54551-6

Melaku, A., & Pastor Ivars, J. (2024). Urban sacred forests support human well-being through cultural ecosystem services. *Journal of Cultural Heritage Management and Sustainable Development.*

Nasirian, H., & Naddafi, K. (2025). A new perspective on climate change in the geography of Iran: current and potential future implications. *Journal of Environmental Health Science and Engineering, 23*(2), 25.

Nathaniel, S. P., & Adedoyin, F. F. (2022). Tourism development, natural resource abundance, and environmental sustainability: Another look at the ten most visited destinations. *Journal of Public Affairs, 22*(3), e2553.

Nepal, S. K., Lai, P.-H., & Nepal, R. (2022). Do local communities perceive linkages between livelihood improvement, sustainable tourism, and conservation in the Annapurna Conservation Area in Nepal? *Journal of sustainable tourism, 30*(1), 279-298.

Nielsen, V. (2025). Public Presentations of Plants: Colonial Legacies and Indigenous Perspectives in the Botanical Gardens of The

Huntington. *Museum Anthropology,* *48*(2), e70009. https://doi.org/https://doi.org/10.1111/muan.70009

Niknam, A., Sarli, R., Taherizadeh, M., Attarroshan, S., & Pourmansouri, F. (2024, 2024/04/25). REDD implementation for greenhouse gas reduction and climate change mitigation in Hyrcanian forests: a case study of the Kojoor Watershed, Northern Iran. *Environmental Monitoring and Assessment,* *196*(5), 474. https://doi.org/10.1007/s10661-024-12616-z

O'Reilly, G. (2020). Cultural Landscape and Heritage Sites. In *Places of Memory and Legacies in an Age of Insecurities and Globalization* (pp. 99-119). Springer.

Olivadese, M. (2025). When Nature Speaks: Sacred Landscapes and Living Elements in Greco-Roman Myth. *Humanities,* *14*(6), 120. https://www.mdpi.com/2076-0787/14/6/120

Orîndaru, A., Popescu, M.-F., Alexoaei, A. P., Căescu, Ş.-C., Florescu, M. S., & Orzan, A.-O. (2021). Tourism in a post-COVID-19 era: Sustainable strategies for industry's recovery. *Sustainability,* *13*(12), 6781.

Page, S. J., & Connell, J. (2020). Urban tourism. In *Tourism* (pp. 443-465). Routledge.

Paing, J. N., van Bussel, L. G., Gomez Jr, R. A., & Hein, L. G. (2022). Ecosystem services through the lens of indigenous people in the highlands of Cordillera Region, Northern Philippines. *Journal of environmental management,* *308*, 114597.

Petersmann, M. (2024). In the break (of rights and representation): Sociality beyond the non/human subject. *The International Journal of Human Rights, 28*(8-9), 1279-1303.

Petriello, M. A., Redmore, L., Sène, A. L., Katju, D., Barraclough, L., Boyd, S., Madge, C., Papadopoulos, A., & Yalamala, R. S. (2025). The scope of empowerment for conservation and communities. *Conservation Biology, 39*(1), e14249.

Rafiei, B., Kioumarsi, H., Amrulloh, H., Ahmadnia, H., Pahmedani, M. A., & Hasankiadeh, Z. K. (2025). Addressing Biodiversity and Sustainability: Challenges and Opportunities in Asia. *Journal of Biotropical Research and Nature Technology, 3*(2), 61-72.

Rezaei, S., Rezaei-Moghaddam, K., Fatemi, M., & Ghafouri, M. (2025). Stakeholder priorities and trade-offs in the sustainable restoration of parishan wetland, iran. *Wetlands Ecology and Management, 33*(5), 73.

Rollo, M. F. (2025). Interconnected Nature and People: Biosphere Reserves and the Power of Memory and Oral Histories as Biocultural Heritage for a Sustainable Future. *Sustainability, 17*(9), 4030. https://www.mdpi.com/2071-1050/17/9/4030

Romagny, B., Cibien, C., & Barthes, A. (2024). *Biosphere reserves and sustainable development goals 2: issues, tensions, processes and governance in the Mediterranean.* John Wiley & Sons.

Rosetti, I., Bertrand Cabral, C., Pereira Roders, A., Jacobs, M., &
Albuquerque, R. (2022). Heritage and sustainability: Regulating
participation. *Sustainability, 14*(3), 1674.

Sadeghi, S. H., & Hazbavi, Z. (2022). Land degradation in Iran. In
Global degradation of soil and water resources: regional assessment and strategies
(pp. 287-314). Springer.

Scheyvens, R., & van der Watt, H. (2021). Tourism, empowerment
and sustainable development: A new framework for analysis.
Sustainability, 13(22), 12606.

Sengar, N., & Shah, S. R. (2025). Geological Heritage Across the
Globe: Importance, Conservation, and Future Directions. In S. Kanga,
S. Kumar, & S. K. Singh (Eds.), *Sustainable Strategies for Managing
Geoheritage in a Dynamic World* (pp. 155-170). Springer Nature Singapore.
https://doi.org/10.1007/978-981-96-3817-8_10

Shahraki, M. Z., Keivany, Y., Dorche, E. E., Blocksom, K., Bruder,
A., Flotemersch, J., & Bănăduc, D. (2023). Distribution and expansion
of alien fish species in the Karun River basin, Iran. *Fishes, 8*(11), 538.

Sharma, J. K. (2025). Ecological and Environmental Crimes: A
Threat to Sustainable Development. In *Transnational Unconventional
Organized Crime: A National and Global Security Concern: Volume I: Thematic
Perspectives* (pp. 55-88). Springer.

Shokri, S., Jafari, A., Rabei, K., Hadipour, E., Alinejad, H.,
Zeppenfeld, T., Soufi, M., Qashqaei, A., Ahmadpour, M., Zehzad, B.,
Kiabi, B. H., Pavey, C. R., Balkenhol, N., Waltert, M., & Soofi, M.

(2021, 2021/01/01). Conserving populations at the edge of their geographic range: the endangered Caspian red deer (Cervus elaphus maral) across protected areas of Iran. *Biodiversity and Conservation, 30*(1), 85-105. https://doi.org/10.1007/s10531-020-02077-4

Siegel, K. M., & Lima, M. G. B. (2020). When international sustainability frameworks encounter domestic politics: The sustainable development goals and agri-food governance in South America. *World Development, 135*, 105053.

Skrimizea, E., & Parra, C. (2019). Social-ecological dynamics and water stress in tourist islands: the case of Rhodes, Greece. *Journal of sustainable tourism, 27*(9), 1438-1456.

Smith, K., Fearnley, C. J., Dixon, D., Bird, D. K., & Kelman, I. (2023). *Environmental hazards: assessing risk and reducing disaster.* Routledge.

Sobhani, P., Danehkar, A., Deljouei, A., Marcu, M. V., & Sadeghi, S. M. M. (2025). Assessing cultural ecosystem services in the Hara mangrove forests: indicators for sustainable management in a Middle Eastern coastal marine protected area. *Ecological Indicators, 178*, 113834.

Sohrabi, H. (2025, 2025/09/01/). Does UNESCO designation enhance forest protection? Evidence from the Hyrcanian national forest inventory. *Trees, Forests and People, 21*, 100956. https://doi.org/https://doi.org/10.1016/j.tfp.2025.100956

Suleymanov, F. (2024). The institutionalization of the Kura-Aras River Basin for effective management of water resources. *International Journal of River Basin Management*, 1-11.

Taekema, S. (2021). Methodologies of rule of law research: why legal philosophy needs empirical and doctrinal scholarship. *Law and philosophy, 40*(1), 33-66.

Tampekis, S., Kantartzis, A., Arabatzis, G., Sakellariou, S., Kolkos, G., & Malesios, C. (2024). Conceptualizing forest operations planning and management using principles of functional complex systems science to increase the forest's ability to withstand climate change. *Land, 13*(2), 217.

Tauro, A., Ojeda, J., Caviness, T., Moses, K. P., Moreno-Terrazas, R., Wright, T., Zhu, D., Poole, A. K., Massardo, F., & Rozzi, R. (2021). Field environmental philosophy: a biocultural ethic approach to education and ecotourism for sustainability. *Sustainability, 13*(8), 4526.

Tehseen, S., Hossain, S. M., Ong, K. Y., & Andrews, E. (2024). Sustainable Tourism in a Changing Climate: Balancing Growth and Environmental Responsibility. In *The Need for Sustainable Tourism in an Era of Global Climate Change: Pathway to a Greener Future* (pp. 69-94). Emerald Publishing Limited.

Trajkovska Petkoska, A., Ognenoska, V., & Trajkovska-Broach, A. (2025). Mediterranean Diet: From Ancient Traditions to Modern Science—A Sustainable Way Towards Better Health, Wellness, Longevity, and Personalized Nutrition. *Sustainability, 17*(9), 4187.

Tseer, T., Ejiofor, P. F., & Marfo, S. (2025, 2025/04/03). Climate Change and Cultural Security in the Postcolony. *African Security, 18*(2), 90-121. https://doi.org/10.1080/19392206.2025.2474272

Upreti, G. (2023). Ecosociocentrism: The Earth First Paradigm for Sustainable Living. In *Ecosociocentrism: The Earth First Paradigm for Sustainable Living* (pp. 307-367). Springer.

Villavicencio Calzadilla, P. (2021). Litigating Climate Change in Bolivian National Courts. In *Comparative Climate Change Litigation: Beyond the Usual Suspects* (pp. 259-276). Springer.

Walia, K., Kumari, Y., Garima, & Mehta, A. (2025). Ecosystem Recovery and Resilience After Forest Fires. In *Forest Fire and Climate Change: Insights into Science* (pp. 119-145). Springer.

Wang, K., & Fouseki, K. (2025). Sustaining the Fabric of Time: Urban Heritage, Time Rupture, and Sustainable Development. *Land, 14*(1), 193.

Wani, M. D., Dada, Z. A., Bhat, W. A., & Shah, S. A. (2025). Community-driven ecotourism in the trans Himalayan region: A sustainable model for cultural and environmental preservation. *Community Development*, 1-23.

Yang, C., Li, M.-Y., Li, T., Ren, F., Li, D.-P., & Chen, L.-A. (2023). Scenic Beauty Evaluation of Forests with Autumn-Colored Leaves from Aerial and Ground Perspectives: A Case Study in Qixia Mountain in Nanjing, China. *Forests, 14*(3), 542. https://www.mdpi.com/1999-4907/14/3/542

Youdelis, M., Nakoochee, R., O'Neil, C., Lunstrum, E., & Roth, R. (2020). "Wilderness" revisited: Is Canadian park management moving beyond the "wilderness" ethic? *The Canadian Geographer/Le Géographe Canadien, 64*(2), 232-249.

Zahed, M. A., Hadipour, M., Mastali, G., Esmaeilzadeh, M., & Mojiri, A. (2022, 2022/04/13). Simultaneous Ecosystem Benefit and Climate Change Control: A Future Study on Sustainable Development in Iran. *International Journal of Environmental Research, 16*(3), 28. https://doi.org/10.1007/s41742-022-00410-z

Zandebasiri, M., Azadi, H., Viira, A.-H., Witlox, F., Jahanbazi Goujani, H., & Iranmanesh, Y. (2023). Modeling ecosystem functions' failure modes: formulating fuzzy risk priorities in the forests of western Iran. *International Journal of Environmental Science and Technology, 20*(3), 2581-2600.

Zhang, S., Xiong, K., Fei, G., Zhang, H., & Chen, Y. (2023). Aesthetic value protection and tourism development of the world natural heritage sites: a literature review and implications for the world heritage karst sites. *Heritage Science, 11*(1), 30.

Zhang, Z., Xiong, K., & Huang, D. (2023). Natural world heritage conservation and tourism: a review. *Heritage Science, 11*(1), 55.

Zuniga-Teran, A. A., Fisher, L. A., Meixner, T., Le Tourneau, F.-M., & Postillion, F. (2022). Stakeholder participation, indicators, assessment, and decision-making: applying adaptive management at the watershed scale. *Environmental Monitoring and Assessment, 194*(3), 156.

Tourism, Heritage Forests, and the Rights of Nature: Pathways to Sustainable Development in Iran

www.ingramcontent.com/pod-product-compliance
Lightning Source LLC
Chambersburg PA
CBHW052137270326
41930CB00012B/2929